D0558887

Mother, Daughter, Sister

T. P. David

Guild Press of Indiana
Carmel, IN 46035

No part of this book may be reproduced or utilized in any form or by any means, electronic or mechanical, including photocopying and recording, or by any information storage and retrieval system, without permission in writing from the publisher. The Association of American University Presses' Resolution on Permission constitutes the only exception to this prohibition.

COVER

"The Brick House" Original watercolor by Jerry Dunbar, WSI Gallery One, Rochester, Indiana.

ISBN: 1-57860-069-3

Library of Congress No. 98-75061

© Copyright 1999 Pond House Projects

This novel is entirely a work of fiction. Although it contains incidental references to actual people, places, and events, these references are used merely to lend the fiction a realistic setting. All other names, characters, places, and incidents are solely products of the author's imagination. Any resemblance to actual persons, living or dead; events; or locales is strictly coincidental.

To all my mothers—everyone from whom I've learned

TABLE OF CONTENTS

INTRODUCTION

I first began to wonder about Matt when she locked Annie in the hen house," Em had said, setting her cup down and getting up from the table.

And Sara had sat without moving, pushing her head against the high, hard back of the kitchen chair to steady herself.

Em had stayed absorbed for awhile, putting the soup on to heat, fixing more tea, cutting slices of cheese, and taking crackers from the jar on the counter, then scrounging for serving containers. It was evident that she usually ate alone.

Sara had been relieved that Em had something to do for awhile. She didn't feel ready to hear about the hen house. Her mind was still on the big kitchen Em had been telling her about.

"Yes, that's when I first started to wonder about her. Matt, that is," Em had interrupted Sara's thoughts again. "Though, at the time, I didn't have any idea things would turn out the way they did, of course."

Sara hadn't replied, still caught up in what Em had told her about the kitchen in the old farmhouse, still wondering why she understood that kitchen so well even though this was the first time she had ever heard anything about it.

"Was that farmhouse brick?" she had asked suddenly.

"No. It wasn't," Em replied. "All frame. Painted white. Dormers upstairs with a small porch on the front and just an open cement stoop, a big one, out back. You went out of the kitchen into the well room, then out of the well room onto the stoop.

No one ever used the front door. No brick on it anywhere. As a matter of fact, I don't think there was a brick building of any kind on the place." She paused, giving the matter some thought, trying to be helpful.

"I suppose the smoke house would have been brick, though," she continued, "because they always were, but I don't remember anything about it. Why do you ask?"

"I was just curious about it," Sara replied. She had been unwilling to tell Em about her nightly visits to the old brick house in her dreams. Still no explanation for that brick house. Anyway, the kitchen didn't sound the same. The kitchen in the brick house of her dream was very austere, more like Em's kitchen, but not the same. Also, Sara spent very little time in that kitchen in her dream, and when she did, she was only doing dishes or tidying up as quickly as she could, so she could go to the attic. She was rarely able to get to the attic in her dream because the stairs were difficult to find and even more difficult to negotiate, but from the moment she stepped into the house, her desire and intent was to go to the attic. She most often woke up before she got there. Her mind returned to the kitchen Em had described and then to her mother and her mother's mother. Sara realized she knew little about her grandmother, and she knew nothing about Annie, her mother's sister, except that she had died as the result of an accident. She had always just lived with her mother's standard reply: "You know I don't like to talk about those things."

Again, Sara's thoughts had been interrupted by Em speaking.

"I've always had a feel for things," Em started out gently. She sat the soup on the table but didn't touch hers. Instead, she took a sip of tea and looked at Sara earnestly. "I can tell you the things as they happened, and then, as they say, you will have to draw your own conclusions."

Sara had only nodded, and she remembered cupping her hands around the soup bowl to draw some of its warmth. She felt inclined to shiver, not because it was too cold in the kitchen, but because she felt that this woman knew the things that could fill in the blanks of her life, things that might help her understand how to move forward with her life now that she had stopped working with the horses, now that she was no longer married, was living by herself, and not required to live up to anyone's expectations but her own. As she sat in Em's kitchen that day, she realized she didn't know what to do next, now that there was no one to answer to but herself.

It had occurred to Sara one more time that she could leave the kitchen right that moment, leave Em's brick house. She could choose not to hear what Em was about to tell her. She could refuse to let the information about her mother come into her mind; she could go on with her life, not knowing. But go on where? She was tired of being stuck in this period of discomfort. No way to go back, certainly, but seemingly no way to go forward either. No, she needed to hear what Em had to tell her. She had to fill in the blanks.

She pushed her head tightly against the old chair again to make sure the present reality was still there, and she recalled the series of coincidences that had brought her to this point. There was the fact that Em, a woman she had never heard her mother mention, was a girlhood friend of her mother's, had even spent a great deal of time with her mother when they were growing up. There was the fact that Em's house was a large, old brick house—very similar to, but yet not quite like, the one in Sara's dreams. And then there was the ad, the ad in the newspaper for the cherry cupboard.

Sara let her thoughts start again at the beginning, trying to get the courage to go on.

THE CUPBOARD

Sara decided to sit in the car a few minutes, feeling a strange reluctance to go inside the house.

"I'm not sure this is a good idea, especially on a day like this," she said to herself as she turned her attention toward the house, or what she could see of it. The light of the morning was that purple-gray light of predawn, when you can't yet tell what kind of day it's going to be. The house itself was mostly hidden from view by a tall and tangled, dense, leafless hedge and rusty remnants of iron fence meshed with undergrowth; however, a cursory look told Sara that, among the vines that covered it, the house was dark red brick.

Almost automatically, she reached for her purse and pulled out the faded sketch. Then she turned and searched the edges of this brick house in the way she searched every large, red brick house she saw. She looked for the tower on the third floor, for the tiny windows with the half-hexagon shaped tops, and for the long front porch with the portico on the left side.

"No, this one's not it," she said aloud, conscious of the fact that she could see her breath as she spoke. She was disappointed but not surprised. She had been looking for the house for the last several years. She always watched for it, wanting to find the exact one, hoping to understand why the strange old house was in her subconscious in such a way that she returned to it over and over again in the night and knew each part of it as if she had lived a whole lifetime there. "No, not it," she said again, huddling by the car door and feeling empty and chilly inside her heavy winter coat.

She sat quietly, hesitating. She was conscious of the sleet hitting the windshield, and she thought of the sleet hitting the canvas tent at her mother's funeral and how everyone huddled against that November wind. The trees were now beginning to show a glaze on their branches from the freezing rain, and she recalled the same glaze on the trees and the little blades of grass underfoot on the day her mother was buried. A strange end to life, to be buried on your birthday, when your own personal part of the world was covered with sleet, she thought.

The car was quickly growing colder with the motor off. "Well, either I'm going in to see this now or I'll have to drive clear back over here." She pushed herself to open the car door, step out, and prepare to find a way through the broken front gate.

Sara gave several strong pulls on the stiff, rusty gate latch and then noticed a missing spoke that was evidently meant to be the place of entry. Turning sideways, she pushed through and surveyed the stark lawn which rolled irregularly and displayed winter-dried grass, alternating with worn patches of dirt. The only accent was one near-barren walnut tree. She looked around again at the thick hedge and began to sense the remoteness of this strange fortress at the edge of town. She noticed that all the front windows were tightly shuttered and that the front entryway was also shuttered and further protected by a padlock.

"Good morning. Really raw day, isn't it?" The voice startled Sara, and she turned to see a stooped woman with streaked gray hair speaking. She had come from somewhere behind the house.

"Yes, very raw day. Very Novemberish. Getting us prepared for winter, I suppose," Sara returned. The woman was scraping at a half-frozen leaf pile with her galoshes, but she kept her large, dark eyes fixed on Sara, peering at her carefully through wire-framed glasses.

"I came about the cherry cupboard," Sara said. "I would like to see it if it hasn't been sold yet."

"Oh, I see," the woman said as though trying to recall. "Yes, the cherry cupboard. I have the cherry cupboard for sale. You saw the advertisement in the newspaper." She looked past Sara toward the barren lawn.

They stood quietly for a few moments in the harsh wind until the woman's attention again returned to Sara.

"Come in," the woman said as she moved onto the porch, evidently planning to take Sara in through the barricaded entrance.

"This house is very old." She stopped her work with the padlock to gaze at the front door as if she had not seen it for a long time. "I was born here in the upstairs front bedroom, the same bedroom my mother was born in." Sara felt her reluctance returning and momentarily wondered if there would be other people in the house.

The woman turned back to Sara. "I don't want to keep you out in the cold," she said as she proceeded to pull the lock off and open the heavy, paint-peeled front door. Sara stepped across the threshold, relieved to be shielded from the Midwestern November wind.

"I need to put a few things in order. I'll only be a few moments. Please have a seat." The woman gestured toward French doors to Sara's left and then proceeded down a hallway toward the back of the house.

Sara looked over the foyer and what she could see of the rest of the house. There was no furniture that she could see. The bare, wide-plank floors and the curved stairway showed evidence of an oiling around the edges many years before, and the centers of the floors were pale, indicating that carpets had once laid there. Long silken tassels that had once supported family portraits or tapestries hung loosely from the ceiling molding, ending at large, cleaner squares on the ochre-colored walls.

Rather balking at the sound of her own footsteps, Sara walked toward the doors her hostess had directed her to and stepped through the opening into a large, empty room. The long outside wall of this room was dedicated to a carved walnut fireplace, flanked on both sides with ornate bookcases built into the wall and reaching to the ceiling. The carved roses and sprites on the mantle were wilted with dust, and no books or ornaments broke the line of the walnut shelving which extended from the fireplace to each end of the room.

Sara's chill returned and seemed to emphasize the room's absolute emptiness. In one corner, by a shuttered window, she noticed the only furniture in the room—a small, round piano stool. She sat on it to wait. With nothing else to do, she began to look again around the bare room and was surprised to feel a faint sense of recognition. There was something familiar here. Something that made her comfortable in this bare room. She sat quietly, waiting to recognize what was going on in her mind.

In a few moments, she began to understand. Surprised that she had not figured it out sooner, she knew what it was. It was the fact that the room had nothing in it. It was empty. That was like her nighttime house. In her dream, the house had nothing in it—no furnishings at all, except for in the kitchen and, of course, the attic. This old house certainly seemed like her dream in that way, but the doors were in the wrong places and the windows were not right. No, this house was not the one.

Satisfied, Sara turned her attention to a break in the slatted shutters, looking outside for some signs of life to catch her interest while she waited. There were no evergreens on the side lawn, and the other bushes had all turned to sticks for the winter. The hedge that surrounded the grounds was evidently barberry, grown into a thick entanglement so that she could see nothing but the upper stories of some of the other, taller houses out on the street. She scanned the yard for signs of life and interest but saw only two small sparrows, who stopped for awhile to peck at the frozen dirt patches on the lawn and then flew on.

Sara continued to wait. Perhaps she waited thirty minutes or perhaps an hour, or maybe it was only ten minutes; time seemed irrelevant in the empty room. She began to think she should let herself out the way she came in, but decided instead to stir around a bit in case the woman had forgotten she had come. Another reason for her unrest was a smaller archway that she hadn't noticed when she came into the room and beyond which she could not quite see from her perch on the piano stool.

The archway appeared to lead to a room at the very center of the house. She grew curious about what might be in that room and whether she might discover what had become of the woman she was waiting for. Impulsively, she stood up, walked over to the archway, and looked through. This center room was absolutely empty, except for the cherry cupboard.

It was even more beautiful than Sara expected. It was small for a cupboard, barely six feet tall, but the brass latches and hinges were glowing with their original luster; and the small square panes in the upper doors were truly old, soft-green tinged, wavy glass. Its finish was warm, waxy red, and Sara knew it was well worth the long wait.

"I see you found the cupboard," the woman said, startling Sara. "I'm sorry to keep you waiting. I was looking for a key." The woman offered this as an explanation, but Sara had the distinct feeling that, for some reason, the woman had wanted her to discover the cupboard herself.

"Yes, I guess I did," Sara said, conscious of the loudness of her voice under the woman's gaze. "I'm very interested in it." She felt somewhat apologetic for her presence in the center room.

"I'm glad you came to see it," the woman said as she moved her hand from the woodwork by the archway and made her way across the open expanse of the center room. "The cupboard is beautiful to look at, but it is the inside that is most fascinating. It's the inside that you will be interested in. Let me show you." She placed her hand gently on the cupboard and began to work with the latch on the upper doors.

Sara had not really looked carefully at the woman before, but now she took time to do so. She had been a tall woman and probably very straight, though now her quite old and well-tailored dress hung much longer on the side of her body that she supported with a cane. Two sweaters, pinned closed over her dress, and the flopping, unbuckled galoshes, still worn in the house, seemed not to detract from her rather permanent kind of elegance.

The woman's pulled-back hair ended in a tight, but very full, French roll at the back of her head. An unmarried woman, Sara surmised, probably a schoolteacher.

"A librarian." She understood that Sara had been looking at her. "I was a librarian right here for thirty-seven years. Never married. Born in this house. I guess I've already told you that, but I've also lived here all my life."

The woman had managed to open the stubborn latch and she turned toward Sara. "Clara Emily Emerson," she said, extending her hand.

"Very nice to meet you," Sara said, grasping the surprisingly strong hand. "I'm Sara."

"Yes, I know. Sara McGalliard. I knew your mother."

Sara skipped the fact that the woman had called her by her maiden name and concentrated instead on what to say next. She was well aware of the fact that not everyone had liked her mother; not everyone had liked Matilda Harvey McGalliard. Best to take a safe route, she decided.

"So you knew Matilda McGalliard?" Sara said, trying to sound as if it were of little consequence to her.

"I never really knew Matilda McGalliard, I suppose," the woman returned. "The person I knew was Matt Harvey. I knew your mother by her maiden name. She and I were friends when we were young. Well, we were friends pretty much until the accident, though we were really beginning to go our separate ways before that." She propped the cupboard door open, ready to show Sara something inside.

Sara responded by putting her head inside the cupboard door to look, but she was well aware of the tightness in her chest and the feeling that she could no longer take a deep breath at the mention of her mother and of the accident. Feeling light-headed, she concentrated on her breathing and focused on the cupboard to restore her sense of equilibrium.

"You see," the woman said, "right here behind this flange is a small lever. If you move it toward the center, it allows you to pull the middle drawer out farther than it would ordinarily come." She demonstrated, then turned to Sara, expecting her to try the combination. Instead, her eyes softened and she said, "You look pale. Are you feeling ill? Would you like to sit down?"

Sara fumbled for words and didn't return her gaze.

"I think I'm fine really," she said finally. "Just a little too much cold air before we're used to it, I guess." Somewhat recovered, she returned her concentration to the drawer and noticed that the back part of the drawer was covered by a lid with a tiny keyhole in the top.

"I wanted you to see this," the woman said, moving her hand

back and forth over the sheen of the small compartment's lid, "but I'm embarrassed to admit to you that I can't find the key just now. That's what I was looking for when I asked you to wait. Sorry to take so much of your time and still not find it."

"That's all right," Sara returned. "If you can't find it, perhaps I could have one made for it, if I decide to take the cupboard."

The woman smiled.

"Yes, you might do that, but that's not all the problem. I have some things in there, some personal things, and I need to get them out before I can let the cupboard go."

Sara was surprised because the rest of the cupboard appeared to be totally empty, and there were all those empty shelves by the fireplace where things could be kept.

"The aggravating part of it is that I just had my things out of there yesterday, so I don't see how I could have mislaid the key very far. Serendipitous, I guess." Both women smiled; Sara knew what she meant.

"Do you have time to sit down a minute and have some tea? Maybe it will come to me . . . where I put it." The woman asked her, and Sara knew that she would.

The kitchen appeared to be the only room in the downstairs of the old brick house that had any furniture, accessories, or bric-a-brac in it, and even that was fairly sparse.

Both women were quiet as Clara Emily Emerson prepared the tea. Sara was surprised to notice how comfortable the silence was, so she occupied herself by looking around the kitchen.

"I've found that I really need very little in the way of things to live very comfortably," the woman said, aware of Sara's assessment of the kitchen. "And that comes from someone who's traveled the world over and collected everything, in addition to inheriting generations of collections. All the shelves, all the rooms—at one time, they were all full." She stopped to look at Sara as if reading her. "What about you? You are interested in the cupboard. Do you have collections to store in it?"

"Well, I have had," Sara returned, "but I have been downsizing for the past year, actually working to be rid of things. Of course, moving into an apartment makes downsizing a necessity more than a choice. After the divorce, I freed myself of many things that seemed to be weighing me down, including my collections. In fact, I even quit my job, which was showing horses, but so far I haven't figured out how to transfer that skill to something else, so I'm just kind of in limbo at the present."

"But I guess moving to an apartment and quitting your job were choices, weren't they?" Clara Emily came back.

"Correct!" Sara was surprised at the woman's perceptiveness. "I see you have been able to do it," Sara continued, anxious to stop talking about her own situation. "You've been able to do the clearing out and still stay in the same place. You've been able to part with things you collected yourself and things that were in your family."

"Actually, I haven't parted with them at all." As the woman paused, Sara immediately thought of the attic. Perhaps the attic of this house was the attic in the old brick house she visited at night.

Clara Emerson noted the look on Sara's face. "No, I haven't stored them all away upstairs to keep from dusting them," she continued, "but I do have each one of them up here." She touched her brow lightly with her finger. "They are all in my mind."

The woman stopped to pour the tea, and Sara sat quietly again, enjoying the aroma of orange and spices.

"Many advantages to keeping them there, actually," she continued. "I can call up anything I want, anytime I want, and I don't even have to budge to do it. I can do it when I'm sitting in my rocker or when I'm fixing tea. I can call up something from Europe or something my grandfather used to milk cows with. I can even call up my mother's wedding dress." She looked carefully at Sara. "Well, I see you get the idea. And it does save on dusting. A few cobwebs up there, maybe," she tapped her head, "but no dust." Both women smiled at this.

"But I'm doing all the talking. I haven't given you a chance to tell me what you want to do with the cupboard."

"I hope you aren't thinking of a beautiful set of china behind those glass doors," Sara responded. "The china went in the first downsizing, along with the expectations it involved. I'm looking for something to hold my books . . . and I don't like to dust either."

"Ah-h-h," Clara exclaimed, then got up to open some of the kitchen cupboard doors. Books were crammed into shelves every which way. "A much more suitable arrangement than those open shelves by the fireplace!"

The books were like a magnet to Sara; she went toward the cupboard to look at some of the titles.

"You certainly have a good collection of Ralph Waldo Emerson and his contemporaries," Sara observed. Just as it came to her, Clara Emily confirmed it.

"Yes, he's one of my ancestors, but not everyone in the family was pleased to claim that. Some of my relatives considered him too far off center, too unorthodox, you know."

Sara could imagine that.

"However, I like to claim him," she stated emphatically. "In fact, I have always been called by the name Em, which my mother considered to be short for Emily, but I chose to think of it as a special connection to Ralph Waldo himself, a little secret I've always had."

Sara was beginning to feel comfortable with this woman.

"I would be glad for you to call me Em if you care to," she continued. "Tell me about your name, 'Sara.' Is it connected to anyone in your family? I don't recall anyone being named Sara in your family, but, of course, I didn't know them all."

Sara felt herself stiffen at the mention of her family again. "No, I don't think so. At least no one ever told me about it."

"What's your middle name, then? Perhaps I would recall it from somewhere."

"It probably seems strange, but I don't have one," Sara replied.

"No," Em said emphatically. "No stranger than Matt Harvey McGalliard. In fact, I think that was just like Matt Harvey, not to give her daughter a middle name. I'm surprised she named you at all, didn't just call you *Girl*. Matt was a leader and a director. One of her better qualities, you could say, but she didn't want to leave any room for being upstaged. Not by anyone, about anything." The older woman's eyes were fixed on Sara. "We stopped being friends shortly after the accident." Em paused a moment, as if weighting her next words. "Tell me, what kind of mother did Matt Harvey

McGalliard turn out to be?"

Sara didn't answer right away. She was torn between wanting to find out the things this woman knew about her mother and not wanting to reveal much about the relationship between her mother and herself.

"Well, there were times when it was fine," Sara started off hesitantly. "Of course, I guess you would know she wasn't your usual Sunday-go-to-meeting mother."

"I'm certain of that."

"But we had the horses together," Sara plunged in. "We rode together a lot. Mother was a wonderful horsewoman. She loved to ride at full gallop. I liked to trot and look around, but she loved to gallop and feel the wind, as she said. The horses are something we had together." She paused here, thinking back. "Mother never showed the horses herself. She thought it was better for me to do it, but she loved getting them ready. That's when we had a great time together. She knew exactly how to make them look perfect, even though they weren't. She taught me everything I know about it."

Sara looked at Em, then continued. "She taught me so much that I've made a good living at it, showing horses for people all over the country . . . a living I've now had the audacity to give up." She looked at Em for a signal to go on. Em nodded and Sara continued. "Yes, I used to be fascinated by the way she could make a horse look to show." Sara paused again. "I guess I know how to do the same thing, now," she said, as if it was the first time she had realized that. "Yes, when she and I were getting the horses ready, it was good. It really was fascinating, the things she could do with a horse."

Em spoke. "There were times when she fascinated me, too. When she was around animals, you're right, she could get them to do about anything. I liked to photograph animals around the farm, and she was often the one who got them into poses for me. I guess the two of you talked about her showing Nightmare at the county fairs when she was a girl?" Em looked carefully at Sara, trying to assess what Sara already knew about her mother.

"I didn't know the horse's name was Nightmare. I just knew he was black." Sara began to feel short of breath again. It was becoming obvious to her that this woman did know a lot about her mother. "Well, anyway," Sara continued quickly, "when we showed horses together, it was good. I always hoped it could just go on like that— that we could just keep showing the horses." Sara ended lamely, feeling that she had already said too much to this woman she barely knew.

"But I guess it didn't," Em said.

"No."

With that, Em abruptly got up from the table and changed the subject, aware of Sara's growing distress. "If you can possibly stay a little longer, I will go upstairs and see if I can find that key. I can't imagine that I would have carried it up there, but I might have."

Sara nodded, and Em disappeared toward the stairway in the front of the house.

Sara sat very still, barely able to breathe again, conscious of the pressure on her chest. She wanted to get up and walk out of the warm, orange-scented kitchen, past the cherry cupboard, through the bare room with the piano stool, out the heavy front door, and across the barren yard to her car. She saw herself doing it. In her mind, she was going through all those places, leaving the old brick house behind. But her body didn't move.

This woman may know, Sara thought. She felt the panic return-ing—the shortness of breath, the dizziness, the numbness in her feet and legs. *She may know about my mother. She may know about McGalliard. She may know what happened.* All at once she felt very tired, and after all these years of wondering, she suddenly wasn't sure she really wanted to know any more about her mother.

She tried again to use her mind to get her body to move. She concentrated on pulling one foot from under the table and placing it out just a few inches. Nothing happened. She began to feel light-headed, so she focused on her breathing, taking even breaths, re-laxing her feet, relaxing her legs, working up her body until the tenseness, the paralysis, began to drain away. Still, Sara sat as if glued in the stiff old kitchen chair.

She knew she was unable to leave. Instead, she closed her eyes very tightly and felt warm tears begin to slide down her cheeks. She sat quietly as she felt the old thoughts returning. She could feel the touching. The touching. Unwanted touching in unwanted places. She could feel it as plainly as the tears she cried this minute, and her body automatically stiffened against it. She leaned her head back again, allowing the pain to have its way and then pass, just as she had so many times before.

"I'm glad to see you're comfortable in that old chair," Em said, seeming not to notice the tears. She had returned and was holding up a tiny brass key. "It's so small, but you just can't get that lid open without it. Believe me, I've tried, because this is the only key I have, and I've misplaced it before."

Em moved in the direction of the cupboard.

Sara brushed at her tears and rose automatically from her chair to follow.

"I could have another key made, I guess," Em commented as she worked with the lock, "but that would take some of the fun out of it. This way, I have to keep track of this one."

The lid to the concealed compartment was open now, and Sara was unsure whether Em meant for her to look in it or not, but her question was answered immediately.

"I'm going to need a little basket or something to put these things in," Em said as she turned to go into the kitchen again, and Sara was left standing in front of the open drawer.

The contents of the drawer seemed to be almost as sparse as the rest of the house: a very worn and oversized deck of cards, a purple velvet bag with some stones spilling from it, and some small, worn books that Sara didn't recognize. Then something else caught her eye. In the bottom of the compartment, almost like lining paper, was a picture of a younger Clara Emily Emerson gazing into a crystal ball.

"It's the other me," Em said, returning with a basket.

The woman certainly had a sense of when to leave the room . . . and when to return.

Sara knew that Em expected her to discover the picture and that she was waiting for her reaction.

"It doesn't seem to fit," Sara said directly. "Your being a fortune teller."

"Do you mean with being a librarian?" Em responded. "Perhaps not. But it fits with being a descendant of Ralph Waldo Emerson, don't you think?"

Sara thought of what she knew about Emerson. "I'm not sure," she started out. "I don't know for sure how being a fortune teller fits in—"

"I'm not fond of the term *fortune teller*," Em countered. "It calls up the image of gypsies and carnivals. Think more about the ability to transcend the ordinary, to tap into a universal energy, to know things without trying to find them out."

"But the crystal ball and the Tarot cards . . ." Sara noted the worn deck.

"Yes, that was how I began," Em said softly. "Sometimes understanding comes slowly and gently. It is not always in the first place you look."

Sara understood that Em meant the comment for her, and she knew now that the woman knew the things she needed to know about her mother and maybe about McGalliard. Suddenly, she felt the need for warmth and the scent of orange and spice and the comfort of the chair with the high back, so she moved toward the kitchen again.

Sara sat down and rested her head against the old chair one more time.

"I do want the cupboard," she said, trying to move herself back into the concreteness of the here and now. "I'll write a check for you when I get a truck tomorrow to pick it up."

"I'm very glad you're going to take it," Em said, looking gently at Sara as if understanding her need to leave. "And, I have something I'd like to give you to put in it. Something from its old home— the first thing you can put in the cupboard when you take it to its new home." She walked to the kitchen cabinet and pulled out a book. It was a copy of *Walden Pond* by Thoreau. Em opened the cover and Sara saw the signature of Henry David Thoreau written in old script.

"This is much too valuable for you to give away," Sara protested. "A signed copy of *Walden Pond*, I just couldn't take it."

"I want you to keep it," Em said. "Anyway, remember, I still have it." She tapped her forehead. "Up here."

Sara didn't feel up to protesting further, so she tucked the book next to her, under her coat, and walked with Clara Emily Emerson past the cherry cupboard, through the bare room with the piano stool, to the heavy front door. Em opened the door to let her out. The women looked carefully at each other, then turned to go their separate ways.

Sara heard the door close as she walked across the barren yard and through the rusty gate to her car.

Inside the car, she sat quietly a few moments, noticing that the sleet had turned to rain. She started the car and turned toward her apartment, knowing very well that she would return to this brick house many times.

THE CARDS

*S*ara was surprised at the transformation that had taken place. Although this day was as gray as the one of her last visit to the old house, a damp snow had covered everything during the night and it had changed the tangled bare hedge into soft powdery designs and had covered the rust on the iron fence. And, as she slipped through the gate, she noticed the vines covering the house had caught the snow in their patterns in ways that made the old place look literally frosted. Even the barren walnut tree had accepted a share of the snow to make a graceful contribution to the scene. Everywhere, this first snow of the season had trimmed things as if decorating for an upcoming holiday.

Sara moved her feet gently through the snow in the side yard as she made her way to the back of the house to enter. She found herself feeling a mixture of excitement and anxiety as she stepped up on the old wooden porch. She was very conscious of the fact that there were things here she needed to know. She stopped for a moment to look up at the third floor, and even though the house was different from the one she visited at night, she wondered momentarily if there was a twisting stairway behind a small, closed door that led to the third floor in this house, too.

"I believe there is understanding here that I need," she said aloud, reassuring herself. Still, she stood quietly on the back porch, unable to lift the knocker.

"How will I start?" she agonized to herself. "I can't just blurt it all out. I can't just say, 'What did my mother do? What was my mother like when she was young? Who was McGalliard? Tell me about the accident. What made my mother act the way she did toward me? How can I reconcile this and get on with my life?' And how much should I tell her about what happened between Mother and me?"

She felt the old paralysis returning. She felt the reluctance to find out, the reflection of her mother on herself. She stood still a few moments and looked out on the snow from the shelter of the porch. The dark, frozen leaves were covered now with clean white snow, concealing the evidence of their deadness and decay; but she knew that when spring came, the soft snow cover would melt and the dead leaves would have to be raked away before the spring grass could turn green and grow and prosper. She had seen enough seasons come and go to understand that rule of nature. So she stood just one moment longer then lifted the knocker and let it fall. She waited for Clara Emily Emerson to answer the door.

"Glad to see you again," Em greeted her. The sweaters were the same, and so were the galoshes. "Beautiful snow, isn't it? Did you get the cupboard situated all right and filled up?"

"Yes, but it looks larger in my apartment than it did in the center room." Sara laughed, taking off her things. "But the great thing about it is, it holds so much. I used both the top and bottom for my books, and I still have some room to spare. I'm really glad to get those books out of the boxes so I can find the ones I want, when I want them."

"And did you find something to put in the center drawer?" Em questioned.

"Well, I gave it some thought, but I don't think I have anything that special or that secret right now, so I'm saving it for awhile."

Em had brewed orange-spice tea again and this time had added some muffins to the repast.

"Those look good," Sara said, settling herself into the high back chair and taking in the pleasant warmth and aroma of the tea as she held the cup close to her chin.

"Thank you, but I certainly can't take any credit, other than knowing where to buy them. I never did learn to cook much, though I certainly came from a family of good cooks. All of them tried to teach me at one time or another. I probably would have had to phone home a lot if I had ever married," Em said, smiling. "I always preferred reading and other things to cooking." She moved around to take a seat in her rocker near the table.

"Do you mean things like . . ." Sara hesitated, trying to decide what word to use. "Well, I don't know what to call it since you don't like the term '*fortune telling*,' but were you interested in that sort of thing when you were a child?"

"I guess we can call it fortune telling for lack of anything better, just now," Em agreed. "And yes, I have been interested in all those things since I can remember. It started with hypnosis, and since I was allowed to spend hours in the library, unsupervised, I read everything I could find on it. Then I wanted to try it out, of course. As you can imagine, my family wasn't keen on being subjects; they just attributed the whole thing to childish whims, so I had to practice on my cat. I actually spent hours waiting for her to get into just the right position so I could work with her. I don't remember now what it was I wanted her to do." Em stopped a few moments, trying to recall and evidently remembering the cat fondly.

"Anyway," she continued, "a few years after I graduated from college, I was able to spend summers in New Orleans, kind of a sabbatical arrangement, and that's where I began to study fortune telling in earnest. Even got to try my hand at it." She stopped for a moment, deciding to clarify. "I was away from home, you know, able to get by with doing some things you can't do in your home town—not if you want to be the librarian anyway."

"So the handbills that were in the bottom of the cupboard drawer came from New Orleans. The picture of you with the crystal ball was made then, the one that says Miss Clara at the top. That was your stage name?"

"Well, that's a little misleading," Em answered. "I never worked on stage. I was more or less understudy for a psychic. Took her appointments sometimes when she had other things to do. And to be honest, I never did understand the crystal ball." She laughed. "But it made a good picture." She stopped here and got up to get the teapot again.

"I do remember spending one whole night gazing into the thing though," she said as she warmed Sara's tea. "Finally, about three o'clock in the morning, I saw a rainbow. I sat looking at it for quite a long time; when nothing else happened, I decided that was a good omen anyway, and that was enough for that night, so I went to bed." She leaned back in the rocker. "Remember, I told you, the answers are not always in the first place you look."

Sara immediately thought of this brick house, the one she was sitting in now, and then thought of the one she visited in her dreams. She thought again of how the downstairs rooms were all empty and of her need to go to the attic, to see what was there, and of the fact that she had started to the attic so many times in her dreams, but the narrow stairs had so many twists and turns it was difficult to get there.

"I loved using the name Miss Clara, though. For years, I enjoyed two parts to myself, always thinking there was no way to integrate them. In the winter I was studious and dutiful and proper, always doing what looked right to others, what was expected of me; then when I went to New Orleans in summers, I allowed my other side to prevail, the part that believes in all things not seen, things you can't touch or feel, energy from outside the material world." Em stopped suddenly, as if she was not sure Sara could follow her any farther.

"Anyway, that's really the only time I used the name Clara by itself. I guess I've always considered it a luxury to have all these names to chose from." She turned toward Sara. "Sara is a beautiful name," she said, "but it doesn't allow you much leeway. I was thinking about that the other day and wondering if you had ever thought of a middle name you would like to have if you could choose one."

"Actually, I have," Sara replied. "It's rather ethereal, and in no way related to anyone or anything that I know. That's why I can really relate to what you are saying about two names to suit the two sides of your personality." She took a long sip of her warm brew. "My other name would be decidedly different than Sara; it would be much more allowing, as you say, to give me a lot more latitude." Sara stopped here, assessing Em's reaction. "It's Aurora," she said. "Sara Aurora. Quite a mouthful isn't it?"

"Ah-h-h," Em smiled and made the same reaction she did when

she held a fresh cup of hot orange-scented tea close to her chin. "Sara Aurora," she said, allowing it to roll out of her mouth like a long, gentle breath. "That is lovely, like a never ending thing, something that goes on and on and on. Yes, a beautiful choice."

Both women sat quietly for awhile, enjoying the warmth of the kitchen and the softness of the feeling between them.

In a few moments, Sara heard herself speaking. "If you knew my mother when she was younger, did you know McGalliard?" she asked, totally amazed at the words that came from her mouth. "I mean," she stammered, "my mother would never discuss it, and I thought you might be able to tell me something about McGalliard."

"I wish I could be helpful on that, but I can't," Em said quickly but gently. "Your mother went away, and she returned home when you were nearly a year old. It was never made clear about who or where McGalliard was." Em stopped as if not wanting to say more. "It was just the way things were done then," she added softly.

"I understand," Sara replied simply. Somehow, she didn't feel terribly embarrassed with this woman, and Em's candid reply about Sara's father seemed to give her courage to find out more. She decided to take a few minutes to draw herself back into the here and now and then figure out how to proceed.

Sara looked around the kitchen, this time studying its sparseness. It consisted mostly of floor-to-ceiling cupboards, tall cupboards with short cupboards on top of them, and, at the floor, the lower cupboards stood on little legs to make room for a person's toes. She noticed that each of the things she had perceived as decorative in her last visit actually served some purpose: utensils for cooking, jars to hold crackers, crocks for flour and spices, baskets for potatoes and dried herbs. She began to realize that though there were few material items in the kitchen, it was far from being drab and lifeless. In fact, it had a decidedly positive warmth and energy. Suddenly, Sara knew how she was going to begin.

"I wonder if you would tell my fortune?"

"I guess we could do that if you would like to," Em replied, and Sara knew she had been waiting for her to ask, expecting her to ask, knowing that she would ask.

Clara Emily Emerson rose from her rocker and came to the table.

She pushed the cups and muffins aside and sat down across from Sara.

"I'm very good at this," she said, looking directly at Sara. "What if you find out things you prefer not to know?"

Sara hesitated, sitting quietly for a few moments, listening to her body, heart, and mind. This time there was no panic, no shortness of breath, no tightness in her chest—just an overwhelming sadness.

"No, I want to know."

Em reached across the table.

"First, I want to see your palms," she said, taking both of Sara's hands in hers and turning them over. "I believe that the lines in your palms, their directions and depth and intensity, tell much about your personality, your inner self. Your palms tell you if you are living in accordance with your inner nature. Just as all fingerprints are different, so are all palm prints. The nuances can tell us much about how you feel about your life now, how it is working for you."

Sara had never paid any attention to her palms before, but now she bent over to look more closely.

"Are you right or left handed?" Em asked.

Sara indicated her right hand.

"In that case, your left hand is considered your passive hand, and it shows the skills and capacities and directions you were born with, while your right hand is your active hand, and it shows the way you are developing those things now." Em paused and looked up at Sara to see if she was able to observe what seemed so pronounced to Em.

"The lines in my hands don't match very well, do they?" Sara questioned.

"You're quite right," Em agreed. "This means that you are not currently living your life in ways that meet some of your deepest needs, ways that are best suited to your true nature. You are resisting the path that is best for you." Em stopped, realizing her words were having an impact on Sara. "In short, you're stuck," she said, trying to lighten things up a bit.

"I can agree with that," Sara said flatly, "but I need to know now what I'm stuck on, how to get out of being stuck, and what directions I need to go forward."

"I believe you know the answers in your subconscious," Em declared, "but you have not yet brought them to the surface."

"They must be really buried," Sara replied, "because I don't have a clue. I guess that was what I was hoping you could help me with."

"I can show you some ways to help yourself," Em said, "but the work to be done is yours."

With that, she went to the basket containing the things from the cherry cupboard drawer, took out the worn deck of tarot cards and fanned them, face down, across the table.

"Concentrate on allowing your mind to be open, allowing any thoughts that arrive just to float through, and very slowly choose some cards from the deck, one at a time. I will tell you when to stop."

Sara concentrated on her breathing, relaxing her feet, then her legs, then her body. When she felt very peaceful and relaxed, she slowly began to pull cards from the deck. Em sat quietly during this time, observing, waiting.

"That will be enough," Em said in a few moments. She took the cards Sara had drawn and arranged them in a pattern in the center of the table. Carefully and deliberately, she turned each one face up, then sat quietly for several minutes, concentrating on the configuration before her.

Sara waited. She sat very still, feeling her breath come into and then leave her body. Even though she said or did nothing, she had the strange sensation that she was communicating with Em in some silent way. She could almost feel her thoughts being transmitted to the quiet woman across the table.

"I believe you have more things to clear out of your life than just a set of china," Em said at last, looking very directly at Sara.

The two women sat for awhile, looking into each other's eyes. Sara's eyes were full of sadness and resignation, as if understanding that she could not avoid the truth any longer, not unless she left the room this minute and never returned. Em's eyes were deep and dark, but also soft and gentle—in the same way they had looked at Sara before, waiting to see if she would have courage, but open and accepting, knowing that it might not yet be time.

"How can you tell that?" Sara said finally.

"Because this card is central to your reading," Em said, holding up an image of the Grim Reaper. "This is often called the Death card by people who are unfamiliar with Tarot reading, but it seldom has anything to do with physical death. It is not that easy, not that clean and clear-cut. It is actually a need to sever something in your mind and spirit. You see the scythe? It indicates the need to cut away the old to make room for the new to grow up."

"Well, I have made several changes lately: moving, downsizing and all, getting rid of lots of old things," Sara said hopefully.

"No," Em said emphatically. "This card is not about material things. There are other cards that deal with that. "Though," she continued, "cleaning out material excess in your life is often an indicator that you are ready to deal with more difficult things. Sort of like getting everything off the kitchen table when you are ready to work on a big project. Setting all distractions aside."

"You mean, while I feel like I've made such progress, I'm actually just getting started?"

"Actually, we're always just getting started," Em returned, smiling. "Even at my age, it may surprise you to know that, every day, I feel like I'm just getting started. I guess the point is whether or not you want to proceed. Not everyone does. It's simply a choice. On any given day, one can choose to proceed or not to proceed. It's a choice we make every day, sometimes consciously, sometimes not."

"What I don't understand is how you knew—"

"No, no," Em interrupted, "I didn't know anything. You knew. You drew the cards. You knew what you wanted to know. You just hadn't brought it to your awareness yet. It was your energy, your deep consciousness that brought up the issue you need to work with."

"But you knew what the cards meant," Sara pursued.

"Yes, but that is only because I have studied the ancient myths and traditions surrounding them," Em countered. "The cards are a beginner's tool, just something to assist you until you are ready to go direct. They have no power in and of themselves. Their only power is to furnish you a gateway."

"What do you mean, go *direct?*" Sara asked. "And what do you mean by *a gateway?*

"Well," Em began, "I notice that you have the capacity to relax yourself, to refocus, to move yourself back to center."

"I'm not sure I know what you're talking about," Sara said, "but if you mean my practice with relaxation, I've been trying to put something I've learned recently into practice."

"Tell me about it."

"Well, there's not too much to tell, except that I had been feeling uncomfortable for awhile, like I was dissatisfied with things, even though I knew I didn't have anything to be dissatisfied with. My life has been running smoothly for quite awhile. Then I began having some trouble with my stomach, but the doctor didn't find anything wrong. I had read some things about biofeedback and relaxation techniques, and I went to take a class in those things. I really think it helps." Sara stopped to consider. "It seems to have helped my stomach anyway, but my restlessness and dissatisfaction continues to crop up much more often than I would like."

She leaned her head back against the familiar chair.

"In fact, it's like something is stuck in me, something I can't put my finger on yet can't get rid of—the proverbial thorn in my side."

Sara leaned toward Em. "I guess that's why I wanted my fortune told and why I'm asking you what you mean by *going direct*. I'm trying to figure out how to get past this block and get on with my life. Sometimes I think I know what it is, but I still don't know how to cope with it. Maybe I'm looking for understanding more than anything."

Em got up from the table and gathered up the cards, placing them back in the basket. She turned toward the stove and put more water on for tea. She stood at the stove and waited, her back toward Sara. Neither woman spoke.

Sara was conscious of a clock chiming somewhere in the upstairs of the house.

The kettle began to whistle, and Em scooped the spices into the teapot and poured the water in. Then she went to sit in her rocker, letting the tea steep.

"Since you have asked me," she said, "I can give you a shortcut, tell you something it took me years to figure out."

She stopped and looked very directly at Sara again.

"That is that there are no shortcuts. There are no cards, no crystal balls to tell you the way. You simply have to live it. But, and this is what makes the difference, you can't live it in the way most people live it. You can't do it mindlessly. You have to be aware of every minute—be in the present, be here now, as the wise men would say.

"Then it comes to you; then you begin to understand it. You can't always be rethinking yesterday or fretting about tomorrow. You have to stay right with each minute, seeing the joy or the agony in it, accepting it all as it comes, the good and the bad—knowing that it moves you forward, that it is part of the learning and growing, that it is part of your evolution, and that your evolution is part of the evolution of mankind."

"Is that what you mean by *going direct* then—no cards, no crystal ball? But what about the things you can't live in the moment? What about things that happened to you before, things that you can't get out of your system or figure out how they fit in?" Sara stopped, debating whether to continue. She looked at Em and understood that Em already knew what she needed to know. All she needed was to have the courage to ask.

"I have a problem about my mother," Sara said with a strange voice that seemed not to be hers. She sat very quietly again, concentrating on keeping tears back. "I'm hoping you can tell me some things about my mother—about her childhood, about when she was a young woman—that will help me understand, help me understand the things that happened between us."

Em rose to get the teapot and pour. Again, the warm, spicy aroma filled the room, and both women held the cups close to them.

"Yes, I can tell you things about Matilda Harvey McGalliard that I'm sure you don't know—in fact, things nobody knows, things nobody saw, things nobody heard but me."

Em took a long, slow sip of her tea.

"But you will need to draw your own conclusions about what those things mean to your relationship with her. What I can tell you may help you sort it out and it may not. And they may be things you would have preferred not to know."

Em sipped at her tea again.

"You understand that I have no particular need to tell these things, because they didn't affect me directly." Em paused, as though giving Sara another chance to stop her. When Sara sat quietly, Em continued. "Though I can tell you that some of the things I saw and some of the things I heard from Matt Harvey herself, gave me pause to think about her sanity. In the beginning, when we were girls, I admired her greatly, because she was a leader. She was a forceful person. She could always devise a plan, find a way to get things done. It was quite awhile before I began to see that many of her plans were devised to manipulate things to her benefit, and it was even longer before I understood that her plans were often carried out at the expense of others. In fact, though, as I said, the incidents didn't touch me directly, I actually grew afraid of her. After the accident, I avoided her completely. Strangely enough, she didn't seem concerned about that even though we had been friends literally since we were born."

Sara leaned her head back against the chair again.

She closed her eyes tightly, trying to feel the security of the warm kitchen, the gentleness and acceptance of Clara Emily Emerson. Her mind blurted scenes from the past into her consciousness and she felt the tears again, but no one could touch her now. She began to feel that the terrible energy that was Matilda Harvey McGalliard was already weakening, was beginning to lose power over her.

"How long has it been since your mother died?" Em asked.

"Five years. Five years this month."

"It's time to move on," Em said simply. "I'll tell you everything I know. Perhaps it will be a good thing for me, too, to bring it back to mind. Perhaps I can gain some understanding now that so many years have passed."

THE BIG KITCHEN

Jenn stuck her feet out from the covers to test the chill before putting both feet flat on the cold, bare floor. She reached to feel Harve's spot in the bed and found it cold. Evidently he had been up for some time, doing chores in the dark, to be ready to harvest when the men came at daylight.

Gingerly, she felt along the floor for her slippers and then pulled the heavy robe over her shoulders and traipsed to the hallway.

"Girls! Girls! Come on now," she called. "I need your help today with all these men. Hurry on up now. We've got lots to do." She grabbed her clothes and headed for the stairway.

Matt uncurled herself from the warm space around Annie's back and slid out of bed, sticking her legs in her jodhpurs and feet in her boots all in one motion. She gave her sister a tug to make sure she was awake, then proceeded to pull on her undershirt and her shirt.

Downstairs in the kitchen, Jenn hurried to lay the base for the cook stove fire: wads of paper and half a dozen pieces of kindling.

"I don't like the look of things till I get this fire started," she muttered. The purple-gray light of predawn always made her uneasy. "This is just the time of day when you can't tell what kind of day it's going to be," she concluded to herself as Matt and Annie creaked out the stairway door and scuffled into the room.

"Matt Harvey. You put her down," Jenn scolded as Matt struggled into the kitchen, leaning backwards, with her arms wrapped around Annie from behind and lifting her so her feet barely touched the floor.

"That hurts my ribs and I don't like it," Annie was complaining loudly as she pulled at her shirtwaist to cover her middle again.

"I don't know what's got into you, Matt," Jenn said, coaxing the kindling. "You keep carrying her around like that, people are going to think you're Siamese twins. Now come on. I need some help here."

The kindling fire was beginning to take the chill off the kitchen now, and Jenn stuck three good-sized pieces of wood into the cook stove to set the fire for the morning. The sureness of real morning light was beginning to make gold tips on the few leaves left on the sugar maple in the backyard.

"That looks better," Jenn said of both the fire and the morning.

The old farmhouse had been in Jenn's family for three generations, and she recalled helping her grandmother cut noodles for hired hands in that kitchen when it was half the size it was now. The kitchen was the best part of the house to her. In fact, it practically was the house—downstairs, anyway. It was Jenn's mother who had the men take down the wall between the old kitchen and the middle room so she had, as she said, "room to cook." Of course, this was done after Jenn's mother's mother and father had reached a respectable age and moved into town to let the next generation have the farmhouse to themselves to raise their family.

Jenn remembered that her grandfather protested greatly, even from his place in town, about the removal of the middle-room wall, and many of the neighbor men joked about turning the place into a cookhouse. But Jenn's mother had her way, and she left this legacy to her only child, a daughter.

The creation of the kitchen left only a parlor downstairs in the small frame farmhouse, and that was sometimes shut off in the dead of winter, so the big kitchen was where the living was done. Jenn was satisfied with this arrangement. She had her rocker near the cook stove; a large, round table and chairs for eating, working, sewing, and lessons; lots of cupboards; and a window above her sink that looked out toward the barns.

"We have to get going here," she said, as much to herself as to the girls, reluctant to interrupt her recollections.

"I'll fix us some oatmeal. Annie, I need crust rolled for three double-crust pies. It's out in the well-room icebox; I mixed it up yesterday. Matt, here's what we need from the cellar. Pay attention now 'cause it's a lot." Jenn hesitated a minute, thinking up her list.

"How's come I always have to go to the cellar?" Matt countered in a grouchy tone.

"I sure don't have time to fuss with you today," Jenn came back. "Anyway, it's the same answer every time. The door is too heavy for Annie to—"

"I can open the door for her and she can go down," Matt interrupted.

"She can't lift the door and she can't carry all these things up. I don't know why we have to go through this every time I need something from the cellar. I don't want to hear another word about it," Jenn stated flatly.

"I'd rather help Dad," Matt continued.

"I'd just as soon you would, too, as much time and energy as it takes me to get you to do anything in here," Jenn said grouchily, "but I have to have some extra help in the kitchen today to get dinner for the men. Now, I'm not talking anymore about it. In fact, you'll probably have to make two trips because I'm forgetting half of what I need."

"Well, I won't go twice."

"You very well may," Jenn said. "Now listen up. I need three cans of cherries and two of apples for the pies, two cans of green beans and two of corn, a can of pickles and one of grape jelly. Be sure to take the basket down with you so you don't drop anything." She stopped to think. "And count the eggs. I don't think there are enough for noodles without gathering."

Matt was picking at a scuffed place on her boot.

"For the last time, get going. I'm out of patience with you, young lady," Jenn snapped and turned toward the cook stove to stir the oatmeal.

Sometimes, it was hard for her to believe Matt was hers—and a daughter, at that. She recalled when Matt was born—upstairs in the farmhouse, with her mother and Doc Whitney there helping her, and with Harve and grandfather downstairs in the big kitchen waiting to see if the first farm child in this generation would be a male. Jenn remembered vividly the pains of labor, but even more plainly, she remembered praying that this child would be a boy so she wouldn't have to go through all of this again. Recollections of the morning nausea came back to her as she stirred the oatmeal. A wonder that she could still look at rolled oats early in the morning, she thought.

She could still plainly see her mother's face as she squeezed her hand and whispered to her, "It's a girl, honey—a beautiful little girl to carry on our line, yours and mine." Jenn didn't know how the news went downstairs, because she went to sleep then, and nothing more was ever said about it. She often wondered how her mother got out of having any more children after producing only one daughter in a farm family. She wished she had thought to ask her. There were many things she wished she had asked her, now that she was raising daughters of her own.

"Is this about right?" Annie interrupted her thoughts to ask her to check the thickness of the crust she was rolling out on the old oak table. She had gotten on her knees on the chair to press the rolling pin heavily on the cold dough.

"I think it needs to be a little thinner," Jenn suggested. "It's kind of hard to do, isn't it—to get it thin—because it's cold. We should have had it out awhile to warm up. But if it's too thick, it will just be gummy when it's done; and when we try to take it out of the pan, it will go limp and all the cherries will fall out. That would cause you and me to have a bad reputation as pie bakers." Jenn laughed as Annie nodded and got to her knees again to work some more on the dough.

Jenn was dishing up the third bowl of oats when she heard the back door slam and stomping feet in the well room behind the kitchen, so she dished up another bowl and set the fourth place at the table. Harve never did like taking off his boots when he came in just to eat. Always figured a good stomping on the rag rug just inside the well-room door "got most of it off," as he said when she questioned him about it.

"Where's Matt?" Harve asked as he picked up the bowl of oats and motioned toward his coffee cup.

"I just took them up. They're really hot," Jenn said, referring to the oats as she set his filled cup on the table. "Matt's in the cellar getting up some things I need to make dinner."

"Well, she better hurry. I need her to help finish the chores and then drive the truck along to unload as we go so we don't waste any time."

"I counted on her in here today." Jenn's voice showed her irritation. "I still have three hens to dress and noodles to make. I thought one of the men would pull the truck up."

"Wastes too much time," Harve said, still standing by the table, scooping in the oats and washing them down with coffee. "Unloading on the go is much faster. I can't waste a man in the truck."

"She's never done it before," Jenn countered, knowing it was a losing battle.

"Do her good," Harve said, and Jenn knew that was the end of the discussion.

Harve was a big man. And if that wasn't enough to help him impose his will, he was the oldest of three brothers, so he long ago developed the attitude that what he said would be the rule. And Jenn had long ago given up anything but a mild protest when she disagreed with him. Instead she found other ways around him when it was important enough to do so; and this time, she concluded, it wasn't. It was taxing her patience more and more to get Matt to cooperate, so just as well she went outside, Jenn reasoned.

Still standing, Harve set his empty cup and bowl on the table, nodding toward the cook stove. Jenn picked them up to refill.

"Aim to break for dinner about 11:30 since we're getting a good early start," Harve said, "but if you don't see us then, you'll know we've run into a problem. Don't bring it out though. Too cold today. The men'll need to come in and warm up. Just look for us when you see us."

Jenn nodded. She was taking in Harve, as he stood by the table drinking and eating. The Harvey boys were raised about three miles away from Jenn's family farm and were known as hard workers and people who minded their own business. In fact, old Mrs. Harvey, Harve's mother, was rarely seen in town; and during the two times Jenn had been invited to dinner with the family after church before she and Harve were married, Mrs. Harvey said very little and basically tended to the needs of her husband and sons and the guest.

Old Man Harvey, as Mr. Harvey was called, was a deacon in the church and rumored to be one of its major contributors. It was well-known how he kept three boys in line and kept their noses to the grindstone, and Jenn suspected, from Mrs. Harvey's demeanor, that the woman was kept in line by the same means, though no one ever said anything about it.

Rumors of the beatings at the Harvey farm concerned Jenn when Harve had asked her to marry him, though there were many things to admire about Harve. He had grown into a handsome man at twenty-one and had basically never had the time or the inclination for girlfriends. He had asked her to attend church with him for Sunday evening services for several weeks, and then proposed marriage. It was as if the appointed hour for getting married had come, and he had looked around for the most likely candidate for a farm wife and chosen Jenn. Both families were pleased with the idea; Jenn's because Harve had been taught the way of a good farmer and was sure to tend the ground well where there was no son to do so, and Harve's because it was a stroke of good fortune to have an oldest son marry a girl who was sure to inherit a farm. So Jenn said yes and dismissed the rumors of beatings from her mind. She never asked Harve about it.

Harve was far removed from raising the girls, considering it his job to provide. Jenn was the caretaker and disciplinarian. He had never laid a hand on the girls or taken a hand to her, so Jenn laid the beating matter to rest, but she often wondered if it would have been different had he had sons.

"What's taking that girl so long?" Harve was just draining his cup when they heard the cellar door drop shut.

"You're going to break that thing for sure if you keep dropping it shut. You've got to let it down easy. Let the weight help you. I showed you how." Harve set his cup down and wiped his mouth on the sleeve of his flannel shirt in the midst of addressing Matt.

"Get your heavy things on. I want you to pull the truck up to unload today."

"I told you." Matt looked straight at Jenn. "I told you I would get to go out."

Jenn let the remark pass, sorting through the basket to see if she had everything from the cellar that she needed.

"What about your oats?" Jenn asked as Harve opened the door between the kitchen and the well room, edging Matt through.

"No time," Harve stated. Then, anticipating Jenn's reaction, he added, "Look at the girl, Jenn. She's sure not starving to death."

Though Matt was only twelve, she had always been big for her age, taking after Harve himself, and had started her periods at eleven, so she was becoming quite developed, Jenn thought, for a twelve year old. She noticed that this change was not lost on Harve; in a way that Jenn was not quite comfortable with, it seemed to add to his and Matt's relationship. Jenn stepped over to the sink to watch them walking toward the barns. There was an uneasy feeling that sometimes came to her anymore.

"How does this look?" Her thoughts were interrupted by Annie's request to check out the first pie she had just finished putting together.

"Really good," Jenn allowed. "In fact, Grandma herself never made a prettier one than that." She gently touched the rope edge around the pie, a trademark of the women in her family. Most women crimped their crusts with a little zig-zag motion, but the women in Jenn's family gave the edge a slight roll between their thumb and index finger to create a design that looked like a small rope around the edge of the pan. Annie had heard the story many times about how her grandma's grandma did it that way, and she had been practicing the edging since she was old enough to play with the dough.

"Yes, it is good. Just as good as Grandma could do," Jenn said, paying Annie an honest compliment and knowing the comparison was one she would want to hear. She touched Annie on the shoulder and then stepped out into the well room to get a pan full of potatoes.

"If you can get those other two finished up just as well while I peel these, then we'll go to get the eggs for the noodles," Jenn said, situating herself in her rocker to start on the potatoes.

The big kitchen was nice and warm now, with the cook stove going and the warmth of the morning sun hitting the south window above the sink. The two women, mother and daughter, sat in pleasant quietness and warmth for some time, concentrating on their chores.

"I don't like chickens at all," Annie finally said matter-of-factly as she finished up work on the third pie.

"Truth to tell, they give me the heebie-jeebies too," Jenn said. "But you like noodles, don't you? Well, I do too so we have to get the eggs." She sat the potatoes in the sink and took off her apron, preparing to bundle up for outside.

"How's come Matt doesn't do it? How's come Matt doesn't get the eggs," Annie countered again.

"Because she takes care of the horses."

"Why does she do the horses and I do the chickens?"

"Well, you don't like the horses much either, do you?"

"No, I don't," Annie agreed, again matter-of-factly.

"I'd say Dad gave her the horses because she's bigger. I expect he plans to give her some cows to take care of pretty soon too."

Jenn and Annie pulled on coats and mufflers from the odd assortment that hung on the rack just inside the back door.

"Is it because I had the fever that I have to do the chickens?" Annie asked as she pulled her rubbers on over her shoes, and the two moved out into the chilly November morning.

"That probably has something to do with it," Jenn offered. "Even if you are only a year younger, you're not as strong since that. Dad doesn't want you in with the horses. It might be bad for your heart. Besides, you're a lot smaller than Matt. You take after my side of the family, a pretty little lady, just like your grandma when she was your age." Jenn knew how to make Annie feel good. She continued, "The women have always done the chickens. I used to help Grandma. Still doesn't mean I like it though."

"I like to feed the cats."

"Well, I don't blame you for that," Jenn agreed. "They're much cuter, but we all have to do some of this."

Outside, the sunshine was sharp against the chill of early November. Annie shuffled through the leaves, leaving a little path in her wake. The last gift of summer, these leaves, to rake into piles and roll in, to jump in, to throw in the air and watch float down.

But soon they would be frozen to the ground.

"I'll go ahead and unwire the gate," Jenn said, "but I won't open the door till you get there."

Annie swiped to the side with her foot to add a new design to her leaf path, and then stopped just a moment to put her hand on her tree.

Her tree was the largest in the backyard. Jenn had told Annie how her mother's mother had planted it when the farmhouse was built, because she wanted a tree halfway between the garden and the house to sit under to clean the vegetables she had picked. Jenn told her, too, how her mother's mother had to move her chair around under the tree all the time, because it wasn't large enough to make much shade, and how Jenn's mother had to move her chair from side to side according to the morning or afternoon sun. But now Jenn and Annie never had to move their chairs to catch the shade, because the tree had grown so large.

When the leaves were full and green, Annie could climb high enough to be hidden from everyone below; and in the winter, the tree was so tall she could see the piles of snow on the branches from her bedroom window. Annie understood that this tree was a gift to her from her great-grandmother, as was the little rope on the pie crust.

"Come on, honey," Jenn's voice broke in gently. "We need to hurry this time."

Annie caught up with her mother at the gate and saw that one hen was still flopping. Its head was about three feet from its body. Jenn saw it too.

"They must have just been here," Jenn said. "That one's still moving."

"I think I'm going to be sick," Annie said.

"Just don't look," Jenn advised. "I thought they did it earlier. Must be running a little late. It'll take three for this big crew though." Jenn made a mental count of the carcasses to be dressed.

"Watch where you step now," she said to Annie, as she moved toward the hen house and waited for Annie to skirt the hens' heads and bodies and trails of blood on her way to the door.

"The main thing I want you to remember about this hen house

when you start doing this by yourself is this door." Jenn lifted the old black latch, pulled the door back against the shed, and shoved a large, round stone in front of it.

"If you don't get the stone in here good, the door can swing shut and the latch will fall in place. Then the hens can't get in to get at the food and water all day."

Jenn had moved the rock into a depression in the dirt then moved it away again, allowing the door to swing shut and, in the process, almost decapitating a hen who had heard the commotion and started out for the day.

"Now let's see you try it," Jenn said. "I want to see if that stone is okay for you or if I need to find a smaller one."

"That stone's okay. I can do it," Annie said as she fiddled with the door latch. "I don't see how this works."

Jenn moved to help with the latch. She said no more about the stone, respecting Annie's need to feel like she was strong enough to do some of the outside chores.

"The latch is kind of hard to open, because it's made to shut when the door swings shut. See." Jenn demonstrated again. "So the hens can't get out at night and nothing can get in to them."

Annie had the latch mastered by now, had swung the door back, and was working on the stone, using all her efforts to push it into the depression. Jenn decided to allow her to struggle and say nothing more about a smaller stone.

"That's good. If you don't get it in the low place, the wind can catch the door and blow it shut. I think you've got it, but I'll send Matt with you a few times to make sure." Jenn checked the security of the stone. "Then you have to fix it the same way when you shut the door in the evening," she said, indicating another depression in the dirt in front of the hen house door.

With that, Jenn shooed two more of the speckled hens out of the doorway and stepped into the hen house.

"This'll be easy for you this time," Jenn observed. "Most of the hens are out by now; we've made such a commotion. It's in the evening, when they're all in here, that you'll get the willies."

Annie stuck her head in the door to spot the remaining hens before venturing into the house.

"I'm never gonna like this," she said again, with resignation.

"That makes two of us," Jenn said, letting out the breath she had been holding as long as she could. "Look, there's three eggs in that nest, and that's all we need to finish the noodles. Let's get those and be done with it for now."

"Good," Annie exclaimed, putting one hand over her nose and carefully picking out the warm eggs to place in the basket. She was anxious to get away from the hen house and back to the kitchen. Walking carefully through the cobs on the floor, she stepped outside and scraped the sides of her galoshes in the dirt.

"You can get through the chicken yard without getting in it sometimes." Jenn laughed. "But you can't keep out of it in the hen house. Might as well wait till you get to the grass."

Annie kept scraping, her eye on the grassy area on the other side of the chicken yard fence.

"I don't think I can carry all three hens with this basket," Jenn said. "You either get the basket or one of the hens." Jenn smiled at Annie as she reached for the basket.

Annie focused on her big tree as Jenn grabbed the headless chickens by the feet and lifted them, blood still dripping from their bare necks, to carry the carcasses to the back of the house. Their heads were left behind in the dirt.

Annie had seen how Dad did it. She knew how he took the heads off the chickens. He always did it early. He opened the door quietly and crept up on one that was roosting. He picked her up around the middle of the body so she wouldn't make much commotion, then he took her quickly outside. Holding the hen's feet, he flopped her down in the dirt and stepped his heavy work boot across her neck and gave a strong jerk all in one swift motion. Blood spurted from the bare neck, and he tossed the body a few feet away from him to flop until it stopped moving.

She never went again, in the purple-gray dawn, to see how the hens were killed, but Matt always did. For an instant, she wondered if Matt had ever killed one. By time to gather eggs in the evening, their heads were always gone, and she wondered who or what took them away.

"I want to try to do two in this bucket before it gets too cool,"

Jenn said as she came out the back door of the house and set the bucket of scalding water on the back stoop. "I'll dip and you pick." Jenn doused the first hen carcass up and down in the hot water then handed it to Annie.

Annie grabbed a handful of feathers and pulled. They came out easily.

"Doing good?" Jenn asked.

"Doing good."

Jenn and Annie always plucked the chickens on the back stoop by the cement, no matter how hot the day. It was as if they had an unspoken agreement not to do this job under the big tree.

In the distance, toward the back of the corn field, they could faintly hear the voices of the men and the clatter of the machines as they silently cleaned the chickens.

"I can dust the noodles as you cut them up," Annie volunteered, thinking ahead to the warmth of the big kitchen.

"Good. That would help," Jenn replied, knowing Annie liked pulling and swishing the noodles through a pile of flour on the table—lifting and swirling them, watching the designs they made in the flour path, making sure all were covered with flour and ready to cook. Making pies, making noodles—a legacy for her daughter, Jenn thought. She knew she wouldn't be able to add on to the kitchen as her own mother had done.

Jenn pulled the guts from the plucked chickens and threw them into a pail, then she headed into the well room to wash down the carcasses, realizing that the bodies would not even be cold when she stuck them in the pot.

"I guess they'll cook faster that way," she said aloud, but just under her breath so Annie could not really hear. Annie had already moved into the big kitchen and was fixing her place at the table to sprinkle the flour for her noodle dusting.

§   §   §

Sara looked across the table at Em and interrupted her. "There's something strange that I want to tell you," Sara said. Her mind was moving so rapidly, she went ahead, not giving any thought to what she was saying or how odd it might sound, no thought to the reflection it might have on her or her family, no thought to how weird she might appear to Em.

"I think there's something important in what you're telling me about the big kitchen. I think there's something about this kitchen here," Sara blurted out. "It is odd to me that I made friends with you. I have trouble trusting women. Generally, I don't make friends with women, but I think it was because of the kitchen. You know how my mother was, so you know what I'm saying when I tell you that I'm afraid to get close to a woman, but there was something different here."

Sara didn't stop and Em made no move to interrupt. "In the beginning, I was afraid of you, I think because I knew you knew things about my family. Yet I wondered why I kept wanting to come back here after I bought the cupboard. I thought it was because I wanted to hear about the things you know, the things you can tell me about my mother; but while you were telling me this . . . about the big kitchen, I also realized I came back because I like it here. I like it here in the kitchen."

Em didn't say anything, and the two women sat quietly, looking out at the soft, silent snow for some time.

"Then you'll need to know what happened at the hen house," Em said finally.

THE HEN HOUSE

J'm taking Matt to town to get her some new boots," Harve announced as he tromped through the kitchen door with Matt close behind. He looked at Matt admiringly. Jenn noticed that Matt was nearly as tall as Harve's shoulder, as they stood there side by side.

"She needs some anyway, and they can be her Christmas present. You can't do chores in the same boots you go riding in when you want to look good, now can you?" Harve pronounced even more emphatically and louder than usual.

"Whatever you think best," Jenn said quietly, still looking at the two of them.

Harve avoided her gaze and went on. "We may just decide to show one of those horses at the fair next summer, and we'll have to look sharp to get anywhere with the judges."

Jenn noticed the difference. Harve never justified to her anything he had decided to do. She was unsure of how to react.

"I wanted Matt to go with Annie to gather the eggs this evening, since she's not used to it yet," she offered feebly.

"Well," Harve said, again in the different voice, "how about Matt taking her out to get her started and then she can finish it up by herself? That way we can get into town before the stores close."

Jenn stared at Harve. Compromise was not something he ever considered. Ordinarily, he would just tell Jenn to take Annie to the hen house herself. Harve still didn't look at her; he focused on Matt instead.

"You can do that, can't you?" he said to Matt. "You can take your little sister out to the hen house and get her started with the eggs for a new pair of boots, can't you?"

Matt made a face but motioned for Annie to come on. Harve turned to go back outside, still never meeting Jenn's eyes.

Jenn turned toward the sink and looked out the window, watching Harve's back as he headed toward the shed where the car was kept. She heard the girls in the well room getting bundled up to go outside. She stood quietly for a few moments then picked up her paring knife and began to peel the potatoes for supper.

"And don't stop at that tree, because I'm not going to wait for you this time," Matt said crossly as Annie trailed behind her out the back door.

"I can't go past without stopping. I made an agreement," Annie called ahead.

Matt turned and came back toward her. She stopped directly in front of her, between Annie and the tree. "And just what kind of agreement did you make?"

Annie looked at Matt and noticed her eyes were squinted angrily above the muffler wrapped around her neck and mouth. She thought about what to say, torn between her loyalty to the tree and her concern about making Matt more angry. Matt was head and shoulders taller than she—and much stronger. She had tried to hold her own with her before but had learned better.

She learned that lesson when she was accidentally shoved down in the manure in the horse barn and when she was accidentally pushed off the ladder in the hay mow and when Matt just walked by her and stamped on her toes and called her Dummy. She doubted Matt would understand her need not to pass the tree without stopping. Not when Matt was already angry about being made to take her to the hen house, even if she was getting new boots.

"And just what kind of agreement would you make with a tree, Miss Dummy?" Matt persisted, still standing in her way.

"Nothing important, really."

"Then come on, and hurry up about it," Matt said, grabbing Annie's arm and pulling her along, making sure she stayed between her and the tree.

"That hurts my arm," Annie protested feebly, trying to cast a sideways glance at the tree from behind her muffler and vowing to make it up to the tree later, when she was on her way back to the house by herself.

Matt finally let go of her arm to undo the chicken yard gate, and Annie rubbed her arm as much as she could through her thick coat sleeve.

"Oh, the hens are already in for the evening," she exclaimed, noticing the empty chicken yard. "That's going to make it hard to get the eggs."

"If you weren't so slow, Miss Dummy, that wouldn't have happened," Matt replied, stomping on Annie's toes.

Annie had known that was coming, sooner or later, on this trip to the hen house. She also knew it wasn't her fault that the hens had gone in a little early on this cold and dreary winter evening, because Jenn had told her about that; but she kept quiet about it, not wanting her cold toes stomped again.

"You do it," Matt said, indicating that Annie should precede her into the chicken house.

Annie shuddered as she stepped through the door. While a few hens were in the nests and on the roosts, most were still pecking at the food and water pans, and scratching around in the cobs. The big rooster turned his head sideways and flapped his wings, not pleased with her intrusion into his territory.

"I'm going to leave now," Matt said loudly from her place just outside the door. "They said all I had to do was bring you down here and get you started."

Annie said nothing. She knew telling Matt that she was afraid in the hen house by herself would not work in her favor. She looked around at the covered windows, boarded up for the cold weather, and realized that the only light was coming through the door, and that it was fading fast. Resolutely, she stuck the egg basket in front of her and headed toward the first row of nests, trying to think of all the things Jenn had told her about how to keep the setting hens from pecking and about not backing the rooster into the corner or getting between him and the door.

The hen house was stone cold, with the exception of the tiny bit of heat that radiated from a group of chickens. It was a very

strange kind of warmth that the group of clucks and feathers radiated; then they would immediately scatter, and the strange little
bit of warmth would be gone. Annie's mind flashed back to dipping
the headless carcasses in the hot water and pulling the feathers out
of the chicken's bodies, and she involuntarily shuddered again.

Annie pulled her mind back to the task ahead and carefully put
the egg basket up against the head of the first setting hen to keep
the hen from seeing her and also to protect herself from getting
pecked by the egg-guarding hen. Basket in place, she reached under the hen's body and groped for the eggs. Two. She carefully pulled
them out and placed them in the basket. She was aware of the chill
of evening settling in the hen house and also of the fact that it was
getting late. She wanted to be sure to be done and safely back in
the kitchen before dark. She moved as quickly as possible down
the line of nests, holding the basket carefully to make sure the eggs
didn't roll together and crack while she used the basket to guard
against the hens. At the same time, she tried to keep her eye on the
position of the rooster. She was doing well so far, she thought, as
she completed the first row of nests with no pecks.

She moved to the second row of nests with her back to the
door, and, somehow, she was aware of what was happening even
before she heard the sounds—a slight and very slow creak, then
the loud thump, followed immediately by the clack. She stood frozen still. She didn't have to turn around to know that the door had
slammed shut, locking her in the hen house in total darkness.

The slam had upset the chickens who were now flapping off
the roost and out of the nests, bumping into her from every side.
The egg basket was knocked from her hand and she threw her
arms up over her head and scrunched down to protect herself from
the claws and beaks and the weight of the flying chickens. She
squeezed her arms as close to her ears as she could to shut out the
terrible clucking and screeching of the distraught hens. Crouching
in terror on the cob floor, she thought about the big rooster with
the spurs on his feet, and tried to squeeze down farther into her
coat as the chickens continued to ram into her in their chaos in
the dark hen house.

Annie didn't move a muscle, afraid to expose any part of herself to the wild pelting. Eventually, she heard the chickens begin to settle down, a few at a time, as they became calmer and made their way back to the nests and the roost. Still, she was afraid to move, hardly daring to breathe in case she would stir them up again. She stayed scrunched down on the cob floor, thinking about the times she had hated even stepping into the litter on the hen house floor. The smell of the litter slowly came into her consciousness, but still she didn't move, even though, after a while, she began to be aware that she was getting very cold.

Jenn heard Matt coming into the well room first, probably while Harve was putting the car in the shed. "She's getting so she makes as much noise as Harve coming in," Jenn said to herself, "and she probably won't take her boots off either."

"Look at these," Matt exclaimed, bursting in through the well-room door and holding one foot up for her mother to see.

"Well, those are really nice ones," Jenn commented, "and black to match Nightmare. You two should show up really well at the fair next summer."

Jenn had never been fond of naming the horse Nightmare, especially since it wasn't even a mare, but the name had been Matt's choice, and Harve agreed, saying that, after all, the colt was all black and a little on the wild side at that.

"See this trim on the top and this side," Matt went on. "This is ostrich. Those little holes are where they take the feathers out of the skin. It all has to be imported, so it's very expensive."

Jenn could practically hear the salesman explaining that to Harve.

"I thought she was going to get the boots for summer, to show the horse. She'll have them ruined out in this bad weather," Jenn chided Harve as he came in the door, the probable price of the ostrich-trimmed boots grating on her.

"They have to be broke in," Harve said plainly and, again, in the rather loud and different kind of voice she had noticed lately. "We wouldn't want her cripping around the show ring with sore feet, would we?" He was looking admiringly at Matt, and Jenn knew the discussion was finished. She didn't ask about the cost of the boots.

"What is Annie doing out there," Jenn said somewhat crossly, making herself change the subject. "It's too cold and dark for her to be fooling around outside. Why didn't you make her come directly in with you when you got home?"

"What are you talking about?" Harve countered, his voice returning to normal.

"She didn't go with us. Matt took her down to the hen house to gather the eggs. Did you take her to the hen house, Matt?" He looked down at Matt, who was sitting on the floor cleaning the dirt off her boots.

"That's where I took her."

"I went there," Jenn said, a sick feeling rising in her stomach. "When she didn't come back in a while, I went down to the gate to see if she was doing all right, but I saw the door was shut so I figured Matt stayed to help her and then she went with you."

"I left," Matt put in, still occupied with her boots. "I didn't stay. You didn't say I had to," she added crossly.

Jenn was already in the well room—getting on her things, getting the light, getting out the door. Harve was close behind. They ran past the big tree toward the chicken yard gate.

"She's been out in this cold over two hours, wherever she is," Jenn yelled, the panic rising in her voice. "See, the door's closed and latched," she yelled again, panting as they reached the gate. "She had to do that from outside."

"No," Harve said, this time very quietly and steadily. "Look at the stone; it's not in front of the door. My God. The door's blown shut on her. Shut her in."

Jenn felt her knees go weak as Harve fumbled with the gate wire with his gloves. She held the light for him to see the latch, but everything began to move in slow motion for her. She was aware of following Harve across the chicken yard, but her own knees didn't carry her. It was as if someone else was in her body, and she was watching the scene from the safety of the big kitchen.

Harve moved the light around the darkened hen house.

"There," he was yelling again. "There . . . by the nests."

The chickens flew into a frenzy again at Harve's yelling, and their bodies pelted him as he grabbed Annie from the cob floor. He tried to put as much of her as possible under his coat. Jenn had her coat off now, wrapping it around Annie's dangling legs, oblivious to the scraping of the claws as the chickens flew madly about her, trying to get their bearings.

Jenn and Harve stumbled out the door with the cold little body—leaving the light behind, leaving the hen house door open, leaving the gate unlatched—stumbling down the dark path they knew so well in the daylight, past the big tree toward the light of the kitchen.

Harve laid Annie on the kitchen table while Jenn fought with her coat sleeve trying to find a pulse. She had her own knees now, here in this kitchen, and she knew what she needed to do.

"I feel it," she cried. "I feel a pulse! Harve, call Doc. We need help here. Then bring that couch in here from the front room. Put it by the stove." She kept her hand on the faint pulse, reassuring herself.

Suddenly, she looked at Matt. She was still sitting on the floor, polishing her new boots. Jenn's mind flashed, but she went on, "Matt, get a blanket and put it in the warming oven. Hurry! Off my bed. Get that one."

Harve was struggling to get the front room couch through the door into the big kitchen. Jenn realized she was unaware whether or not Harve had reached the doctor.

"He'll be right here," Harve said in a stiff voice. "He was at home. He'll be right over." Jenn knew he was trying to keep himself from sounding worried.

Harve picked Annie up and laid her gently on the couch. Jenn never let go of the faint pulse, holding it tightly with one hand while she adjusted the afghan from the front-room couch around the cold child with the other, still waiting for the blanket from her bed.

By the time Doc Whitney arrived, Annie had already opened her eyes and begun to stir a little.

"A little while longer and it would have been a very close call," Doc was saying in his gruff voice as he checked Annie over, trying not to unwrap her more than necessary. "You did the right things, warming her slowly," he addressed Harve and Jenn. "Don't look like there'll be any permanent damage. Staying curled up may have saved her some fingers and toes." He looked at Annie and said, "You'll be fine in a day or two, young lady," again gruffly but with a pat on her shoulder, as he prepared to leave.

Later on, when supper was finally over and Annie had taken a little warm broth, and Harve and Matt had gone upstairs to bed, Jenn pulled her rocker over by the couch next to the stove in the big kitchen and sat quietly next to the sleeping Annie. She began to go over the evening's events in her mind, trying carefully to recall whether there had been any wind that evening; but, soon, relief and exhaustion overtook her and she fell into a heavy sleep.

§   §   §

When Em finished speaking, both women sat quietly in the semi-darkness of the kitchen. Only a small light on the stove cast a slight pattern through the high back of the unoccupied chair onto the table.

Sara spoke first. "So Matt was never punished?"

"What could she be punished for?" Em answered. "It was accepted that the wind blew the door shut. Matt told me all about it herself. Just as she told me in great detail about Nightmare nearly stepping on Annie in the horse barn and about the time Annie slipped on the hay mow ladder. Matt relished telling me those things. In the beginning, I thought she exaggerated them to get my attention, but I came to be less sure of that."

"Do you think Matt shut Annie in the hen house?" Sara asked.

"I didn't at the time; I thought she just wanted me to think she did. But eventually I began to think differently." Em sounded almost apologetic toward Sara.

"It's all right," Sara said. "I want you to tell me everything. I need to draw my own conclusions." She paused a moment. "But I want to ask you this: Why do you think Matt would do something so cruel to Annie?"

"Of course, at the time, I wasn't sure she did—still don't know absolutely," Em replied. "But it could have been because Jenn was closer to Annie. Jenn and Annie were turned more alike."

"Yes, but Matt was closer to Harve," Sara countered.

"Well," Em looked down at her hands, "it's hard to tell exactly what the nature of that relationship—the one between Matt and Harve—was."

"I see," Sara said quietly.

"I'm going to look for something," Em said, sounding relieved that Sara was not upset with her and glad to change the subject.

"Upstairs, I think I have an album with pictures of your mother and Annie when they were girls, before the accident. I used to spend quite a bit of time there and I think I have pictures you would be interested in seeing, pictures of Matt and Annie."

"Good. Yes," Sara replied, "I really do want to see them if you can find them. I have seen very few pictures of my mother, almost none from that period of time, and I only recall ever seeing one picture of Annie. I came across it in a box of my grandmother's things, and then I never was able to find it again. Never found the box at all again, actually. And I did look for it after Mother died. I have to tell you something curious, though. She still had those boots. She told me she got them as a young woman, when she used to go riding. Certainly before I was born, she said. I can tell from your description that they had to be the same ones. In fact, I always thought they looked a little small for a grown woman, but I never thought to question her about it. She didn't like questions, you know."

"Strange that she saved those boots," Em agreed. "But I know she did wear them for years."

"Well, I'll hunt out that album, and we can look at it next time you come over," Em said, getting up from her chair. Sara thought Em looked much older tonight, and very tired. Suddenly it occurred to Sara that Em might be unburdening her life at the same time she was Sara's.

The two women said good-byes, and Sara made her way around to the front of the house and through the rusty gate space to her car. Once inside the car, Sara sat in the quiet, feeling the cold. She closed her eyes and saw her mother's angry eyes, felt the stomping on her toes, and heard the words *Miss Dummy*, just as if she were a child again. She felt the warmth of her tears on her cheeks as she pulled away from the old house and headed for home.

THE ALBUM

Sara sat down on the floor of her bedroom and pulled open the bottom drawer of her chest. Carefully, she lifted out boxes without stopping to open them. She knew what was inside each of them by the size and color. She stopped for a moment at the old red Christmas box from her favorite department store. The corners were split and taped many times where she had taken the lid off to look at the pictures—pictures from her marriage—looking for clues to why it didn't work out, why two people who were of such different orientations would try to make a marriage anyway. It was another issue she had yet to figure out.

Today, she didn't open that box but sat it aside, going deeper into the drawer, looking for the box that probably was once white but had now turned brown around the edges, the box that had yellowed pinkish roses in the center of the hinged lid. When she came to it, she took it out of the drawer with a certain feeling of gentleness toward it that she had not experienced before.

She sat it down on the floor and waited quietly before opening it, trying to connect with the young woman who had opened that box so many years before. Gently, she lifted the lid and began to take each piece of the old celluloid dresser set from the box. She was strongly aware that she had never looked at the pieces this way before, especially when she saw the little note left inside, written in a hand that wanted her to remember:

*To my daughter, Jenn
On her sixteenth birthday
With love, from Mother*

She had often seen the note written to her grandmother when-ever she looked through the drawer of special things, but now she felt she was a part of the woman who had written it and the woman to whom it was written.

First, she lifted out the mirror and looked at her reflection as she sat cross-legged on the bedroom floor. She looked deeply into her eyes to see the other women there, the ones who had come before her: her mother, her grandmother, her great grandmother. Perhaps there was a pioneer woman, weather-wrinkled before her time; perhaps there was a black woman, eyes dark with slavery; perhaps there was an Indian woman with strong and stormy eyes. She sat for a few moments, seeing them all, feeling them all.

Next, she took out the nail buffer, worn thin. No doubt that her grandmother had enjoyed using that. She looked at the odd little dish with the lid and the hole in the top—a hair receiver, she had been told. She examined it more closely and realized that there were still a few hairs in it.

"They must be my grandmother's. They must be Jenn's," she said aloud astonished that she had never noticed them before.

She carefully replaced the lid and cupped her hands around the little piece, much as she did a warm cup of tea that Em prepared for her. Slowly, Sara got to her feet and took the old, pale-green celluloid comb and brush to her dresser and sat down. She looked at each one. The brush was completely flattened with use, but Sara took the comb and began slowly and gently to comb her hair. She sat at her dresser for a long time, noticing the sunshine reflecting in the mirror, combing her hair with her grandmother's comb, and feeling her connection to the women before her.

It was nearly eleven o'clock when she realized she had told Em she would be there in time to have lunch before they began going through the album.

"Sorry I'm a little late," she apologized as Em opened the door on the back porch.

"I went through some old things to find a dresser set that belonged to my grandmother, Jenn, and I kind of got lost in thinking about it. In fact, I sat down at my own dresser and used the comb. As many times as I've looked at that dresser set, I've never actually used any of the pieces before—or even touched them, for that matter." She decided against saying anything about the hairs or the eyes in the mirror. She didn't want Em to think she was going off the deep end with this thing.

"Was it a green celluloid set with a hair receiver?" Em asked. When Sara nodded, Em continued, "It was a birthday gift to Jenn from her mother, and I remember that Matt and Annie were asked not to use it because it was something special. Only thing in the house that I can remember that we weren't supposed to handle. Of course, that made it all the more interesting to us, so we went in to look at it every now and then. Also because it had a button hook with it, and none of the newer sets did. It seems like I remember that it wasn't new when Jenn's mother gave it to her. Maybe it had been in the family before or something."

Sara thought about the eyes in the mirror.

"Well," Em continued, changing the subject, "as I told you on the phone, I found the album that I thought you would be interested in. I haven't looked in it yet myself. Thought I would wait until you came so we could enjoy it together; however, it may take me some time to remember about some of the things that are in it."

Em began to set things out on the table: bags and bowls from the refrigerator. Obviously, lunch wasn't the important matter of this day. "I have made us some hot tea, though," she said rather apologetically as she poured.

"I want to tell you how this album came to be," Em started out. "I went to spend several weeks of the summer with Matt when my folks took a tour, as they were called then, out West. I don't remember just exactly why I didn't go, but I think it was because they went with some friends, another couple, who didn't have any children. At any rate, I had been interested in photography at that stage, and my father got me a new camera to practice with while they were gone, saying he expected to see that I had improved my skills by the time they got home. He always encouraged me to be interested in things, and I must say, he indulged me or suffered through most of my interests, so I don't recall being offended at not going on the tour. At any rate, I made this album of pictures, taken just during that period of time, to show my father."

Neither woman had touched the lunch as they took long sips of tea and turned their attention toward the album.

The first several pages were pictures of horses and a cat, with some obvious attempts to get the cat in certain positions and sometimes even dressed in doll clothes gone awry. Both women laughed at this. There were close-ups of the big black-and-white cat from nearly every direction, in doll buggies and doll beds, and with its head stuck through a doll house window.

"I can't believe now that I put that poor cat through all that," mused Em. "I'll bet he was glad when that summer was over." She turned to the next page.

"Ah, I was beginning to think there was nothing for you in here, but here's one you'll be interested in," Em said, pointing to a picture of two teenage girls holding baby kittens.

Sara didn't take long to recognize the older one as her mother. It was Matt as a young woman. Sara stared at the picture, realizing how much Matt looked like her father, Harve—just as Em had described to her. She also recognized that Matt had on jodhpurs and boots, even though she was seated. Em sat quietly, and Sara looked for a long time, trying to see something that would help her understand the woman that was her mother at this age.

"Is this you?" Sara asked finally, referring to the other girl in the picture, unable, again, to get a reading on the girl that was to be her mother.

"Oh no. I was always taking the pictures," Em replied. "That's Annie. I guess you haven't seen many pictures of her. Everything about her was just kind of put away after the accident. As you said, your mother wouldn't tolerate questions about her, and everyone said Jenn was never the same." Em stopped here and studied Sara's face. "This is probably the last picture taken of her before she died," she continued gently.

Sara looked at the younger, smaller girl in the photo. She was in the image of Jenn. Sara immediately felt the sharpness and the heaviness of her grandmother's loss.

"I guess you can see why one of the girls belonged to Harve and one belonged to Jenn, can't you?" Em interrupted her thoughts.

"Yes, I certainly can," Sara replied.

Em got up to fuss with the teapot, fixing more tea, giving Sara time.

Sara stared at the younger, smaller girl in the photo. So this was Annie, she thought. She looked at the way she held the kittens in the lap of her skirt. She looked at her hands and arms, at the buttons and tucks on her shirtwaist, at the square of her shoulders and the cut of her hair. She looked at the set of her chin. She looked at the line of her mouth and the curve of her cheek. Finally, she looked deeply into her eyes, and she felt an odd and very sharp connection to her.

"I would like some more tea when it's ready," Sara said quickly, frightened by the intensity of the feeling she had just experienced.

"Just ready," Em responded, coming to the table with the steaming pot. Sara quickly turned the page in the little album to see the next cat antics.

"This will probably be remembered as my animal period of photography when these are famous," Em said, laughing but sensing Sara's need to move away from the picture of her mother and Annie.

The women took long, warm draughts on their tea as they encountered more pages of animals in odd poses.

Sara was beginning to calm down again and feel that she had seen all she needed to see of the little album when the next page caught her full attention and caused her to take a sharp breath. She stared incredulously at the big, dark, brick house with the porches and the tower she had seen so many times in her dreams.

"What house is this? Where is this house? Who lived in this house?" Sara asked with her finger on the picture. She was asking questions faster than Em could answer.

"It's the house they lived in when these pictures were taken," Em replied.

"Nobody ever told me that," Sara said, agitation in her voice.

"I thought they only lived on the farm; that's all my mother ever said."

"Well," Em replied, "they only lived in that house one summer. Harve's aunt had died and he was in charge of the estate—a sizable one, people said—so Harve rented that house in town for the summer to be near the bank and the lawyer and to dispense with his aunt's properties, as I recall. I was too young to know or care much about why they were living there, but I do remember that we girls loved it because there were no furnishings on the second floor. We had the run of the place, used to fantasize all kinds of things up there. Took old curtains up there and pretended to be queens. We were in our early teens, but we still had our imaginations. Children grow up so fast now—"

Sara interrupted impatiently. "Do you say there was no furniture?"

"Well, there was furniture on the first floor, but not a lot because it was sort of a temporary living arrangement you know." Em was somewhat surprised by, but attentive to, Sara's sudden and intense interest in the old brick house. "No, there was not a stick of furniture on the second floor," Em continued. "We used to talk Jenn out of some chairs to take up there sometimes to enhance our imaginary goings on."

"I would just like to sit and study this picture for a little while," Sara said.

Em sensed the seriousness in her voice and nodded. She pulled a plate toward her and arranged some cheese and crackers to go with her tea, then took a knife to peel an apple. Neither woman had eaten a bite yet.

Sara looked hard at the photo. It crossed her mind briefly that this was the second picture in this album that had caused her mind to jump, and, for a brief moment, she felt as if she were combing her hair again. Turning her mind back to the picture, she scrutinized every detail.

The porch was deep and seemed to start around one side of the house, stretch clear across the front, and end in a portico on the other side of the house. The main door of the house was at the side, and the front of the house was centered by bowed glass windows—

just as she had seen so many times in her dream. The windows on the second floor echoed the first-floor windows in shape, being tall and slender. But it was on the third floor, under the eaves, that the shape of the windows caught Sara's eye. There, the windows were shorter to accommodate the roof line, and the tops of these small windows formed a half-hexagon shape.

Sara closed her eyes tightly, seeing the dreams, thinking about the times she wanted to go to the attic in the old brick house, thinking about looking up the small, crooked stairway. When she was able to make enough turns on that stairway, she would see the small window at the top, the window with the half-hexagon shaped top.

"What was in the attic? What was on the third floor?" she asked Em, surprised at the strange and faraway sound of her own voice.

"Nothing," Em replied. "It was empty too. Jenn didn't like for us to go up there because she thought the floor in the tower part might not be substantial. We had the whole second floor at our disposal so it really didn't matter that much. Annie was the one who went up there most of the time, because Matt didn't like for her to hang around with us." Em stopped here and looked thoughtful. "That always surprised me because Annie generally didn't disobey Jenn. But what would happen is that Jenn would let us all go play on the second floor, then Matt would pick at Annie and she would just go off to the third floor by herself. It was really more of a third floor than an attic, though the eaves were kind of low, if you see what I mean," Em pointed to the picture. "Anyway, Annie would just go off to the third floor. When we were ready to go downstairs, she would go down too. I guess she thought it was safer than tattling on Matt's behavior."

Sara's mind was catapulting back and forth between what Em was saying and her dream; all this mixed in with the strange sense of already knowing what Em was telling her. She felt a little bit crazy, like her mind was flitting back and forth in time.

"I've dreamed about this house," she finally blurted out. "I've dreamed about it many times. That's why I found this house you live in so interesting when I first came here. I was trying to figure out if it was the one—the brick house in my dreams. I knew it didn't look exactly right, but there was no furniture, and that was like my dream, so I kept trying to make it fit."

Sara realized she was feeling short of breath, but she rushed ahead. "What else can you tell me about the house inside, especially the third floor? Do you remember about the stairs to the third floor? Was there a small door that had to be opened to get to them, and did the stairs have a turn? Do you remember if you could see one of those little windows when you reached the top of the stairs on the third floor?"

Sara was glad she was sitting down, because her body felt weak all over. At this point she leaned her head back against the chair and closed her eyes to calm herself down.

Em studied Sara quietly a few moments before she answered, then she spoke very carefully, slowly, and calmly. "I don't recall much about the third floor, as Matt and I didn't often go there. Only Annie did." Em looked very directly at Sara as she said this. Sara felt as if the blood was draining from her body, and the two women sat, quietly looking at each other for a long time.

"As I recall the house, it is much as you have described in your dreams," Em said finally, still looking intently at Sara. "I wish I could answer your questions about the third floor, but I can't." Again, Em was quiet; she continued to look at Sara as if deciding what to say next. After a long pause, she spoke.

"Do you know where this house is?" Em asked.

"No," Sara replied. "I have been watching for it for years. Every large, dark, brick house I see, I always look at it carefully to see if it's the one."

"Your mother never said anything about it then, I guess." Em knew where this was going to go eventually. She hesitated, then said, "It's over in Fulton. It's still there now if you want to go and look at it. They've turned it into a county museum of sorts, but I don't think they have made any structural alterations, so you could probably get some of your questions answered by going over there and looking at it."

"In Fulton?" Sara said incredulously. "I can't believe no one ever told me about it. I can't believe I never came across it myself. In Fulton. Only a few miles from here. I can't believe it."

"Well, it is a little off the beaten path, out on the west edge of town, kind of to itself. You wouldn't have occasion to go there unless you wanted to do some county history research. Librarians always know about those things," Em said as lightly as possible.

"But why didn't anyone ever tell me?" Sara questioned. "Why didn't someone tell me that a house they lived in was just in the next county?"

Em was quiet again for awhile.

"It's the house where Annie died," she said finally.

Sara's mind began to blur. She couldn't say anything. She felt as if she couldn't move. Her legs were heavy and her body was heavy in the chair. She saw her vision start to blur and she closed her eyes and began to take deep breaths, to concentrate on her breathing to keep from passing out.

"I'm right here," Em said. "Take all the time you need."

§   §   §

Again, Sara found herself sitting in the car for some time before going toward this old brick house. She had circled the house several times before stopping, looking at it from every angle. Now, she was no longer afraid that this wouldn't be the house; she was afraid that it was.

She once more scrutinized every detail from the seeming safety of her car. The porch and portico were right; the entry door was right; the tall, bowed windows downstairs were right. There were even more details that could not be denied. The house was fronted by an iron fence, and the walk leading from the gate to the porch was laid with huge slabs of stone. The stone slabs leading to the house were a detail she had forgotten from her dream; she was reminded of them by reality.

"Sometimes I'm not sure which reality I'm in," Sara said to herself.

She turned her head to look down the street the other way. She could see cars passing on another street in the distance, and it gave her the feeling of getting her bearings again. For a moment, she wished she had accepted Em's offer to come with her to see the house, as she wasn't sure she could get up the courage to go in by herself. From looking at the outside, she was sure what she would find inside. Even though she had never been in the house before, never even seen the house before, she knew just where the doors were positioned; she knew about the fireplace with the marble cherubs; she knew about the window seat beneath the bowed front windows.

Sara felt herself shaking, and she sat quietly again with her eyes closed, breathing deeply, trying to calm her body so she could move. Eventually, she felt ready, and she opened the car door and felt her legs, legs that really didn't feel like her legs, moving her up the stone slab walk toward the house.

"Nice to have you visit us on this chilly day," the old man said as he opened the ornate front door. "I'm the caretaker and curator here. Lived in this area all my life and always been interested in the history of this county. Now, the man who built this place back in 1887 was Colonel Ephraim Rufe. He was not a native of this area, but came here from New Orleans shortly after his stint in the Civil War. He was from New Orleans himself and was a procurement officer for the Confederacy. Had a lot of wealth that he saved by sending it up North during the war.

"Anyway, the house is full of imported things, things brought over from Italy and brought up the Mississippi on barges just for this house. The old Colonel knew how to get what he wanted, being in procurement." The man smiled at his thought of the colonel's shrewdness. "Brought black folks, too, to help take care of the place. He was a slave owner down South before the war, but he paid these black folks. We have a file of receipts for their wages . . ."

Sara wished the man would be quiet, but he continued talking, so she nodded and smiled appropriately as she looked around the room. She saw the series of three windows set in a protrusion in this room and she knew that this must actually be the dining room and that the main entry to the house must be somewhere else. She noticed the tall ceilings with ornate moldings and the heavy paneled pocket doors. It occurred to her that she had regained the sense of her legs belonging to her body. She was, in fact, beginning to take for granted that she knew in advance what she would see if she moved to another part of the house. The man was still talking nonstop, so Sara decided to interrupt.

"I am mainly interested in the house itself, more so than the history. I wonder if I might look in some of the other rooms?" she inquired, noticing the impatient sound in her voice.

"Sure," the man said, though he looked somewhat disappointed as he pushed open the tall pocket doors so that Sara faced a huge room with a fireplace in one end, flanked by tall curved windows.

Sara walked immediately to the fireplace and ran her fingers over the smooth, cold scrollwork of the marble mantle. She looked for signs of alterations, but could find none.

"Has the house been altered much?" she asked, interrupting again.

"No," the man replied in a pleased tone. "This house is built on pieces of quarry stone, cut and set into place. It's never even settled. All oak trim. Probably couldn't pry this thing down if you wanted to." The man was off on another explanation of the advantages of old-fashioned construction as Sara tried to edge her way toward the next set of pocket doors, hoping that she could enter another room. The man, still talking, didn't move. Sara interrupted again.

"I had been told there was a fireplace with some beautiful cherubs carved on it here some years ago. Do you have any idea what could have happened to that mantle piece?" she asked.

The man stopped talking for a moment and pushed open another set of the huge pocket doors to the next room.

"Still here," he said proudly. "I told you they couldn't pry this place apart if they wanted to." He walked over to the fireplace on the side wall of this room and patted the soft green of the marble cherubs' heads affectionately. "Seven fireplaces in this house. All of them still work, but of course we don't use them. Too dangerous. This was the most expensive one. We have some of the receipts from the building that the old colonel kept."

The man continued talking, and Sara put on her smile and nod while she looked around the long room. She realized that in addition to the cherubs on the fireplace, the end of this room was filled with the bowed windows that one could see from the street. Beneath them, built in a curve to follow the windows, was a window seat.

Sara felt herself growing more excited. She interrupted again.

"I have some interest in the third floor," she said impatiently, "the floor with the tower. Do you suppose I could go up there?"

"Well," the man said, his face clouding, "we keep that shut off. There's nothing up there and so we don't heat it. Don't heat the second floor either. Just down here."

"Then I wonder if I could just see the stairway that goes up there," Sara said.

She realized her voice had a pleading note, and the man was now looking at her quizzically.

"I guess we could go that far," the man said, evidently wanting to accommodate her strange request. "Wait till I get my coat."

As he disappeared toward the rear of the house, Sara was relieved to finally have some quiet to try to get a feel for the house. She walked over to the window seat and sat down. She looked across the broad porch onto the front lawn and across the stone slab walk. She was making a mental note to come back in the spring and sit in this spot again, just as the man returned to the room. "Better turn up your coat collar," he advised.

The man opened a door to a broad front entry hall, showing Sara a massive curved stairway to the second floor. Excitedly, she started up with her host trudging along behind. When she arrived at the second floor landing, she immediately faced another open stairway to the third floor.

"Is this how you get to the third floor?" she asked, disappointment in her voice as she recalled the small, dark, enclosed stairway behind the door in her dreams.

"Yes, but you can see we've put a piece of plywood up there at the landing so no heat goes up." The man was trying to be patient.

"I would like very much to see the third floor," she said resolutely. "I can help slide the wood over. I see it's not nailed in place." She paused, then added, "You see, I think my relatives may have lived here once," hoping that was enough to convince him, but not to generate questions.

"It would be better if you could come back in warmer weather," the man said feebly. But he saw that Sara meant to see the third floor today. "Well, I can scoot the wood over myself," he resigned. "It's not that heavy. Watch your head now."

Sara moved her body through the space provided and saw that there was a broad landing hall with four doors leading off it. The third floor had rooms in it just like the other floors, except the ceilings were much lower and the windows were small, tucked under the eaves and dormer-like with half-hexagon shaped tops. She stood at the top of the stairs and looked around. From that point she could see into each of the four rooms and could see several of the small windows, but none was prominent. None faced directly to the top of the stairway.

Sara turned her attention again to the stairway, looking straight down the opening to the second floor.

"Is it possible this stairway has been altered over the years?" Sara asked.

"No, no, not at all," the man said, and Sara noticed he was beginning to shiver in his light jacket. He had been quiet for the last few minutes.

"Are you sure?" she pushed.

Now the man was the one who was growing impatient. "Yes, I'm sure. Look at this stair railing," he said with an effort to keep the crossness from his voice. "It is an exact match to the one that goes from first to second floor. Same wood, same workmanship, same aging. There are no cuts, no alterations anywhere. Also, look at the floor around the landing here. No sign of alteration." He said this last emphatically, as though realizing he had to convince Sara quickly if he hoped to get back to the warmth downstairs.

"I will just take a quick peek in each of these rooms, and then I'll be ready to go down," Sara said, disappointed that the stairway was not as she had pictured in her dream but also feeling apologetic that she was keeping the man up here in the cold.

She stepped quickly and glanced into each bare room, noting in particular the room with the square tower offset. She saw the four little windows in the tower that matched the rest of the windows on this third floor, then she reluctantly turned to go back downstairs.

Both she and her host were quiet as they slid the plywood back into place and then traversed the two stairways back to the warm part of the house.

I'm making a fool of myself about this dream, she thought.

"I'm really sorry to drag you up there in the cold," she said aloud and apologetically. "It's just that I had a different kind of stairway pictured." The words just kind of fell from her mouth. "I was thinking of a narrow one, enclosed, with a door." She couldn't believe she was babbling on this way. At least she didn't say she dreamed of the narrow stairway. "I guess I was picturing the third floor stairway more like an attic stairway." She forced a little laugh. "Must have been in some book I read as a child." She was beginning to feel a little strange about this whole thing herself.

The man took off his jacket and laid it across the desk. He looked at Sara and then sat down. He moved some papers over on the desk and then looked at Sara again.

"There is another stairway to the third floor," he said, "in the back part of the house. In my quarters. It was the servants' stairway back when the colonel built the place. It goes to the second floor then on up to third." He anticipated Sara's next question by the look on her face.

"Yes, I can show it to you," he said.

Sara didn't even remember to thank the man, but headed directly for the door marked private that led to the rear of the house. That door led to a hallway with assorted doors on each side. The man walked first through an open one that was his kitchen and poured himself a cup of coffee.

"I'll just let you go on up by yourself." He nodded to a door across the hall. "I need to warm up here; that stairway is too small for both of us anyway."

He sat down at the table with his coffee, and Sara turned toward the door he had indicated. It was the smallest door in the hallway—not tall like the other doors which were proportioned for the high ceilings, and it was narrower than the others, too. She opened the door and felt for a light switch. She could see six narrow, steep steps and then a wall where the stairs evidently made a turn. She moved carefully up those stairs and turned to face another short flight of steep stairs with a door at the top. She opened the small door when she reached it. She looked around and realized she was on the second floor of the house. She turned back to the stairway and proceeded up the next short flight to the landing. She could barely make out the last short flight of stairs, as she had not thought to look for any more light switches. To make matters worse, her knees were getting weak again as she started up this last flight, and she felt the need to touch the stair passage wall for support. She stood for a moment when she reached the top, her hand on the knob of the small door at the top of the stairs. She was aware that she felt clammy inside her winter coat.

Sara felt her head beginning to swim as she turned the knob to pull the door open. Directly in front of her was an unobstructed view, across a bare room, out one of the half-hexagon shaped tower windows.

MATT AND ANNIE

After her visit to Fulton, Sara had moved her grandmother's dresser set from the bottom drawer, taken it from the box, and placed it on her own vanity where she could look at it and touch it and use it every day. This morning, it was gray and raining but not at all cold, the first promise of the coming spring.

A little February break in Indiana—when you know there is winter left, but you know that the spring will come soon, Sara thought. *Just as it always has and always will.*

As she looked tenderly at the marbled green comb this morning, she thought about the other women and the other springs. She thought about gathering eggs and about making pies in the big kitchen she had never seen, and she realized she had the sense of it all, here in her apartment on a rainy February morning. She looked again at the small, green dish and the lid with a hole in the top, and again she looked inside to make sure her eyes had not deceived her, that her grandmother's hair was still there.

She picked up the nail buffer and looked at the place that was worn through. Did a farm wife spend time buffing her nails? Or had that been worn before, when her grandmother was still a young woman without the responsibility of eggs and meals and daughters to raise? Perhaps it was worn down by a previous owner, someone in her great grandmother's family, or someone no one in her family even knew, but a woman, living her own particular life in the ways women had before her. Sara picked up the green comb and ran it slowly through her hair, thinking all the while about opening the small stair door and seeing the hexagon top on the window in the tower.

Anxious as she was to get into the house and tell Em about what happened when she went to visit the brick house in Fulton, Sara decided to sit in the car for a few minutes, listening to the rain before she went in. She consciously recalled that first time she sat in the car in front of Em's house, debating on going in to ask about the cherry cupboard.

She sat quietly a moment, feeling the coincidence of answering that newspaper ad. She thought of sitting in the car that first day, listening to the sleet and remembering her mother's funeral. She looked outside at this gray day and noticed the difference. A difference between November and February in Indiana. Now the rain was no longer preparing to freeze things but, instead, washing them, cleansing the earth for the bloom of a new season. She looked at the lone tree in Em's front yard and saw the tight, dark, red buds just perceptible on the tips of the branches and twigs.

"Yes," she said aloud. "It's on its way." And with that she pulled up the hood on her raincoat, got out of the car, and hurried through the broken front gate toward Em's back porch.

"I've been anxious for you to come," Em said, opening the door as Sara came around the back corner of the house. She had evidently been watching for her to arrive. "I know it was nothing we wanted to discuss over the phone, but I thought these two days would never pass. I want to know what your impression was from the house, what your feeling was about being there."

They moved into the kitchen, still talking. "I can tell you that I was tempted to come directly here after I had been in the house," Sara said, "but it was getting late in the day and there were too many things I wanted to ask you. We would never have gotten to bed that night." Sara laughed. "Besides, it was a mind-boggling experience, and I needed to digest it for awhile before I could talk about it."

Sara took off her coat and hung it on the rack by the back door.

She turned and looked directly at Em. "I knew all about the house. I knew how the windows were arranged. I knew about the tall pocket doors, and I knew about the cherubs on the fireplace. I also knew about the back stairway to the third floor," Sara said seriously. "I knew all about it as if I had lived there many years ago. It made me feel strange. I sometimes felt like laughing and sometimes felt like crying when I was in there, but my overwhelming feeling was one of awe. Awe that I was there *again*." Sara stopped and repeated, "Awe that I was there again, Em. It was like going home."

Both women stood looking at each other and neither spoke. Finally, with a gentle look in her eyes, Em took Sara in her arms and hugged her. "I'm not surprised," she whispered in Sara's ear.

Nothing more was said for awhile. Sara sat down in her chair by the old kitchen table, and Em prepared the tea kettle for their customary tea.

"I guess you know that I'm going to want to know everything you can possibly tell me about the summer in that house," Sara said finally. "I need to know everything that happened there. I especially need to know everything about the accident and Annie's death."

She proceeded to tell Em, in detail, about her visit to the house. Em interrupted often with questions of her own, as if sharpening her memory for the work ahead. Finally, she sat down at the table.

"As much fun as we had with our own imaginations," Em began, "we were beginning to be conscious of the changes in our bodies at that age. We were also beginning to become boy conscious." She stopped to think a minute. "Not so much Annie, as she was kind of small for her age and not developing much yet, but certainly Matt and I; we were both good-sized girls and beginning to look like young women."

Em stopped again, wanting to choose her words carefully, and yet to be careful not to leave anything out.

"In fact, we discussed at length ways we could better our chances of attracting a beau, as we called them then." Again, Em stopped. This time she looked up softly at Sara. "You're certain you want to hear all these things?" she asked gently.

"Yes," Sara said. "Everything." There could be no qualifications now.

"Well, then," Em continued, "it was early in the summer, and we girls were not used to being in Fulton around more young people, you know. There was a young man a few blocks away who could drive an auto, and that was quite an attraction back then. We speculated on how we could attract his attention. I think we were enamored of going out for a ride in the car with a boy, not really thinking so much of becoming his girlfriend, certainly not realizing that only one of us could be that." Em paused again and got up to put more water on for tea.

Sara sensed that Em was reluctant to tell her the things she most needed to know, so she got up from her chair and went to the stove to stand beside her. She put her hand on Em's arm. "I'm asking that you tell me these things," Sara said. "I need to find my way through things, get some peace of mind for myself." She stopped here, then decided to continue. "I don't think it was any accident that you put the ad in the newspaper to sell the cherry cupboard. I don't think it was any accident that an antique cupboard was the only piece of furniture that I have considered buying recently, a cupboard to hold my books. I don't think those things were a coincidence." Sara was looking at Em in earnest. "I don't think those things were accidental, do you?"

"No. I've lived a long time. I've seen a lot of things. I've studied a lot of things. It was not an accident that we met," Em said.

"Then we have to trust each other now. You have to trust that you can tell me things exactly as they were, and I have to trust that I can tell you things that I'm trying to resolve regarding my relationship with my mother."

Sara was surprised that she could say this last without becoming short of breath or feeling lightheaded. "I need to know, and you are the only way I can find out." She looked directly into Em's eyes. The two women sat down at the table again.

Em started out hesitantly. "That summer was the first time I became aware that Matt was sometimes purposely hurtful to Annie . . . I mean physically. I had seen her tease Annie until she cried, and she often called her names, but not having siblings myself, I thought that might just be part of it. It was early that summer that I began to think differently." Em stopped for a sip of tea, and this time Sara sat quietly, knowing she would continue.

"It was really quite a warm day for mid-May," Em said, "and, as usual, the three of us had gone to the second floor to make-believe and discuss girl things. It was so warm that we had taken off our shirt waists and were left with just the top half of our skivvies—that's like an undershirt—on our upper bodies. We were sitting on the floor in a circle in the room that faced the front of the house. Things started out by our discussing how we might attract a beau, as we were inclined to do at that time, and we were discussing our names. The whole thing seemed innocent enough, and, for a change, Matt had not chased Annie off to the third floor yet."

§   §   §

"I think you would do a whole lot better if you would have everyone call you Emily instead of Em," Matt said. "It's too much like Emma, that woman down at the grocery, or worse yet . . . it could remind people of an enema."

The three girls laughed at the reference to the dread consequence of irregular bowel movements.

"I don't think I could get used to 'Emily' now," Em countered. "It just sounds too . . . well, too persnickety to me. Emily doesn't sound like someone who ever has any fun."

"Well, we're not talking about having fun here," Matt came back. "We're talking about how we can get a ride in that car. 'Em' may sound like having fun to you, but 'Emily' sounds like a Gir-r-r-l."

"Do you have any ribbons for my hair?" Em said, hopping up, putting on a coquettish look and prancing around the room. The girls laughed.

"I think Em's a good name," Annie ventured. "Besides, what difference does it make what your name is. If people like you, they like you. If they don't, they don't. I can't see that having a fancy name makes any difference."

"What would you know about it, Miss Dummy," Matt snapped suddenly, evidently angered that Annie had entered into the discussion with her own idea, particularly since it disagreed with Matt's. "You've never had to worry about it. You have a good name. *Annie*— that sounds like a girl and a sweet little good girl at that."

Matt had gotten to her feet now and was scowling at Annie's challenge, which was something Matt certainly didn't tolerate well. Annie continued to sit on the floor, looking down.

"How would you like it if you were named *Matt*, and everyone always thought you were going to be a boy. How would you like that?" Matt was bending over now, trying to talk to Annie's face.

"Well, you could be called Matilda, if you wanted," Annie protested feebly, "after all, that's your real name."

"Oh, Matilda, Matilda!" Matt called out sharply, walking around the room with the back of her undershirt pulled up over her head like a babushka. "*Matilda* sounds like a washer woman. Matilda, put the cat out. Matilda, bring up the cows. Matilda, put some wood on the fire! No, I don't think so, Miss Dummy. I don't think I would want to be called Matilda." She was leaning down into Annie's averted face again. "Although you would probably like that, because then I could do all the work around here. Not that I don't anyway, since it's always too hea-a-avy for you!"

Em began to be uncomfortable at Matt's rage, and when Annie started to speak again, she wished she would not say anything more.

"You know we were named after our great aunts," Annie spoke. "I had nothing to do with which name I got."

"Then let me ask you this," Matt was still talking to Annie's down-turned head. "Why weren't you named Annabelle? That's what our aunt was named! Matilda and Annabelle Lee!" Matt was yelling now. Em was growing very uneasy, but she was afraid to interfere.

"I can answer that!" Matt continued talking loudly. "It was because Mother didn't want people to think you were a steamboat, so she shortened it to *Annie*, didn't she? She shortened it so you got a nice name!" Matt's face was red from anger and bending over, and

Em prayed Annie wouldn't say anything, but she did.

"You know Mother thought it was funny to tell us that story," Annie was saying timidly, her head still lowered. "She didn't mean to give you a bad name."

"Do you think I don't know she likes you best?" Matt continued her tirade. "*Annie, let's bake pies now . . . Come on Annie, I'll help you gather the eggs,*" Matt shrilly imitated Jenn's voice.

"But you like to be out with Dad," Annie continued to try to counter Matt's rage, and Em watched in awe. She had seen Matt's temper, but not to this degree and not over something of so little consequence. "Besides, you were born first so you got the first-choice name." Annie was speaking a little more loudly and defiantly now, but her head was still down. "Anyway, I told you, I don't think it makes any difference what your name is. A boy will either like you or he won't."

With that last remark from Annie, Matt dropped down to the floor and stuck her face in front of Annie. "What would you know about it anyway?" she shouted. "And what do you keep looking down there for? You haven't got anything to see!"

With that, Matt grabbed at Annie's chest where her breasts would someday be and pinched with both hands as hard as she could. Annie squealed in pain and wrenched away, then ran toward the stairs that led to the third floor.

§   §   §

When Em finished speaking, she looked down at the table, feeling unsure that she had done the right thing in telling Sara about this episode.

Sara didn't speak for a long time. She noticed her teeth were still clinched tight as they had been while she was listening to Em recount Matt's actions toward Annie. She had moved through the story with Em word by word, anticipating the outcome, knowing what the outcome would be, feeling Annie's emotions and pain with every action Em described.

"Did Matt get punished?" Sara asked finally.

"Annie didn't tell on her, I guess."

"And you didn't say anything?" Sara asked without accusation in her voice.

"No." Em was looking directly at Sara now. "But, I wished later that I had. You can believe me when I say there have been many times in my life that I have thought about it and wished that I had. Things might have gone differently if I had. I can tell you that I have given all these things thought, in retrospect, over my life-time."

Em got up and walked over to the window to look out at the early spring rain. She stood for awhile, then turned to Sara again.

"If we can get through this . . . if we can trust each other enough . . . if we can hear the recounting of this, it will help us both. It will be as helpful to me as it is to you," Em concluded.

"Yes," Sara said. "I want to know." She understood the older woman's need for reassurance that they should continue.

Em sat quietly for a long time. She kept both hands around her tea cup, drawing on its familiarity, its warmth, its comfort. After a while, she spoke again. "There were other things," she said, "other things that summer. The things you want to know about." Em looked up at Sara, and Sara saw that her eyes were filled with tears.

Em looked down at her hands around her cup. "As I told you, that old brick house was a temporary living arrangement for your grandparents and the girls—they rented it just for the summer—so there wasn't much furniture. Matt and Annie shared a bed, just as they did at home out on the farm. But there was a difference. Out on the farm when I stayed overnight with Matt, Annie was sent to sleep in the spare room. In the brick house, there were no spare rooms so all three of us girls slept in one bed that summer. Well, you understand . . . I mean, there were plenty of spare rooms; they just didn't have any furniture in them."

Sara began to feel strange in the old way. She began to feel short of breath and lightheaded. She knew Em was stalling, and she knew why. Sara knew what she was about to hear.

Em looked at Sara again, very gently and for a long time, and then she continued. "With three of us in the same bed, we had to sleep close together. I am a very sound sleeper, so it took me quite some time to realize what was happening." Em stopped and took her hands away from her cup and put them in her lap, holding them tightly. Sara could see that Em was starting to shake.

"Matt slept in the center," Em's voice was shaking, too, "and she always curled herself around Annie's back. I slept on the other side with my back to them, facing the outside of the bed so I would feel like I had more room, being used to having a whole bed to myself." She stopped again, trying to gain composure.

Sara sat, staring at the rain running down the window pane, and waited.

"Sometimes Annie would cry out in the night," Em went on, "and I would wake up because her cries sounded hurt or afraid. But if I stirred, Matt would always just say I should go back to sleep. She would say that Annie had bad dreams."

Em continued to shake, and Sara continued to stare at the little streams running down the window.

"But after while, I had trouble sleeping. I had a feeling that it wasn't all right. That what was happening was not all right. It was mid-summer by then, and I kept remembering what Matt had done to Annie upstairs, and there were other things I had seen her do. Ways she touched Annie . . . ."

Em stopped again, and Sara wondered what Annie did when Matt touched her in those ways, but she wasn't able to say anything; no words would come out.

"I couldn't always sleep," Em said with a certain finality, "and I knew that Matt was hurting Annie in ways she shouldn't be." Em looked down at her clenched hands in her lap. "But I didn't say anything."

Neither woman spoke. Sara was conscious of her mind beginning to blur and her vision going dark. She closed her eyes tightly and tried to concentrate on the sound of the rain hitting the window to shut away her feelings, but the sensation of her mother against her back, of the groping hands, came to her anyway as she sat, not daring to move a muscle. Unmoving . . . unmoving . . . unmoving . . . .

The rain could still be heard, but it could no longer be seen when Sara opened her eyes and saw that it had turned dark outside. She felt the back of her head against the high back of the kitchen chair, and she realized she must have been sleeping for a while. She turned to look and saw that Em was still sitting next to her, eyes closed. The tea kettle was on the table now and still warm, so Sara guessed that Em must have made fresh tea and stayed nearby as Sara slept. Sara poured some warm tea into her cup and then sat quietly, allowing her mind to rest. She kept her head against the back of the chair, as if to help her remember where she was. The kitchen was as dark as the outside now, with the exception of the little cooking light on the old stove.

Sara looked around her at the jars with the crackers and beans, at the tea strainer and the familiar utensils hanging on the wall. She looked toward the tall cupboard doors and thought of the books behind them. She thought of the book Em had given her, the book that was at home in the cherry cupboard. She wanted to see everything that was familiar, everything that could remind her to be in the present, to be here now, to remove herself from the past and live and breathe in the present. She called up one of her favorites from the old Zen wisdom:

Before enlightenment, chop wood and carry water.
After enlightenment, chop wood and carry water.

It gave her comfort to know that others before her had discovered that no matter what things happen to one externally, there is a center that one can return to—imperturbable, calming, a center in the self.

Cautiously, she allowed herself to begin thinking. She thought about combing her hair with her grandmother's comb, and she thought about the giver of the comb, her grandmother's mother. She tried to feel their presence, the women before, to guide her now. She closed her eyes again and began to think about Annie. Annie, who died young and baked pies and hated chickens. She allowed Annie's feelings and presence to fill her mind and spirit, and she sat with it for awhile.

Eventually, she dared to turn her mind to Matt. She thought of Harve's attention to Matt and perceived his strange love for her and his . . . well, you had to call it lust for her. She allowed Matt's anger to come into her mind—anger at being perceived as a boy, at not being her mother's favorite—and she felt the surprise of the warm tears on her cheeks as she let Matt's pain flow into her mind.

Sara kept her head against the high back of the chair as she felt the flow of the women before her passing through her mind, as she listened to the early spring rain washing against the window pane just as she knew each of them had done.

Em stirred, and Sara looked across the table at her.

"Thanks for sitting with me all this time," Sara said simply.

"I knew you needed to rest," Em said, "and I guess I did, too."

Em got up to get the jar of crackers from the counter, and she took a can of peanut butter from the tall kitchen cupboard.

"It's gotten late," she said, busying herself with paring and coring an apple to add to the peanut butter repast. It was evident that neither woman quite knew what to say next, so they spread peanut butter on crackers and cut pieces of apple and sipped tea.

Finally, Em spoke. "How do you feel?" she asked. "I mean, how do you feel about learning these things? I know you have told me you wanted to know, but actually hearing them said may be a different matter." Em paused for a moment. "I am concerned about how you can receive these things. But I sensed that you were ready, that you already knew some of it and just needed it confirmed." She stopped and looked at Sara. "I also think that you are ready in spirit, that you have prepared yourself to know the past while moving forward with your own life."

"I am surprised at how I feel," Sara said quietly. "Of course it may be that I'm numb, but I feel just as you say, that you have only confirmed things I have been dealing with for years in the back of my mind." Sara took a long draught on her tea and leaned her head against the chair again. She looked at the shadows cast by the little light on the stove. "In the back of my mind, but always present—always present, always nagging for awareness, always nagging to be dealt with, always nagging to be understood." She sat quietly again for a few moments. She looked at her teacup then picked it up and took a small sip. "I feel relieved, Em."

"Well, if that is the case, then I think we should continue," Em said earnestly. "There are things about the accident, more things I think you will want to know, things that will have meaning to you." Em poured herself more tea. "That is, if you want to hear them." She stopped again and looked at Sara. "Why don't you think it over for a few days and let me know. If not, we can certainly find plenty of other things to discuss."

With this last, Em got up from the table, and Sara understood it was time for her to leave and for both women to get some rest.

"I'll let you out through the front tonight so you won't have to walk around the house."

The two women walked through the bare rooms toward the front of the house, and it occurred to Sara that the absence of things, the openness of the rooms was actually comforting to her. As they reached the front door, Em put her arm around Sara and looked at her tenderly. "Be careful," she said.

Sara pulled the hood of her raincoat over her head, conscious of the patter of the raindrops, and made her way to the opening in the rusty front gate. As she settled herself behind the steering wheel and prepared to begin the drive home, she felt like it had been years since she climbed out of the car this morning.

THE BOYFRIEND

*S*ara took a long time with the morning paper. She sat at the table feeling the warmth of the sun on her back through the window and her old, terry cloth robe. In a while, she picked up the picture of Annie that Em had sent home with her, and she began to study it. She looked at the small square shoulders and flat chest covered with a shirt with tucks and a row of tiny buttons. She looked at the square shape of Annie's face and the smoothness of the straight bangs and the chin-length bob that surrounded it. Annie's nose was finely chiseled and her eyes were small, but Sara looked closely and she saw the light in them, shining out of the faded old photograph. She looked long and hard into Annie's eyes, then suddenly got up from the table and went toward her bedroom.

When she returned, Sara had a picture of her grandmother, Jenn, in her hand and laid it next to the photo of Annie. She saw the same smallness but also the same squareness in the two women, the same set of the shoulders, the same set of the chin. The mouths were different, but the eyes . . . the eyes were the same—small and deep set, but a speck of light sparked out from the centers. Sara sat for a few moments, transfixed, looking from one set of eyes to the other, understanding the connection between these two women, this mother and this daughter.

Sara rose from the table again and went to her bathroom where she picked up the soft-mottled green comb, a comb that she was sure would have been given to Annie . . .had she lived to use it.

Sara held the comb tenderly and then began to run it through her own hair again.

Sara blinked as she stepped out into the late-March sunshine. She hurried toward her car, pulling her coat close around her to shield herself from the biting wind. She was conscious of the warmth of the sun through the car windows as she drove toward Em's house, and she was conscious of the bushes and trees and ground—bare yet, but anxious to bloom. She looked for the smallest hint of spring-time: a crocus leaf, the first bud on the forsythia. They were not to be seen yet, but she could feel their closeness, the readiness of the coming season.

Em met Sara at the back door.

"Guess what?" Em started out. "Today, we have a real lunch."

Sara looked toward the table and saw the same hodgepodge of dishes as usual, but this time there were no jars, cans, or boxes on the table.

"I hope you're hungry, because I think I have enough to feed a half dozen of us. Everything looked so wonderful, I just couldn't help myself."

Sara had taken her customary seat, and now Em was placing beautifully prepared dishes on the old oak table. Some came from the refrigerator, some from the stove, and some from the tall cupboards.

"This is beautiful!" Sara exclaimed. "Where on earth did you get this?"

"I notice you ask me where I got it," Em said, smiling. "I guess that means there's no question in your mind that I got up in the wee hours to prepare this lovely lunch for us?"

"Well-l-l-l," Sara hedged, and both women laughed.

"I had an appointment in Kokomo early this morning to take care of some business with my attorney. I always prefer to use an out-of-town attorney, so I can keep my private business private. Well, anyway, I had often seen this ethnic deli close by, so, since I was having a guest for lunch, I decided it would be a good time to try some things out."

Sara was surprised on two counts. First, she never thought of Em going into the nearby town. In fact, she never thought of Em anywhere but here in this house. Secondly, she never thought of Em having business to take care of. The whole idea of Em being out of these familiar perimeters flustered Sara.

"Do let me help you on this. You have spent more than a week's groceries here," Sara blurted out, aware that it wasn't the most correct thing to say, but taken aback by the jolt in her perception of Em. "It's such a beautiful lunch," she added, trying to make a weak recovery.

"Thank you for the offer," Em said gently, "but there's no need. This is just a little something special for you and me."

To pass the awkward moment, the two women turned their attention to the delicate carvings of the colorful kiwis, oranges, and cherries made into flowers and the intricate arrangement of cucumbers and tomatoes into geometric designs.

"That certainly is a skill, to be able to turn ordinary-looking fruits and vegetables into works of art," Sara commented.

"It's a mother and daughter deli," Em said. "Well, really, a mother and four daughters, if you can imagine that. And Mother must be every bit of eighty, but bustling around, right in the thick of things. A very small woman, but she has an authoritative voice." Em paused and smiled. "It was pretty loud in there. A mother and four sisters. How else could it be? A great, busy, productive atmosphere," she finished, musing over the family enterprise.

"Well this food is all certainly as good as it looks," Sara added, now recovered from her earlier embarrassment.

Em pushed her plate away and picked up her cup of tea. She looked at Sara. "I didn't sell the things out of the house because I needed the money," she explained.

Sara wasn't sure what to say, so she just sat quietly, waiting for Em to continue if she wished.

"It was because I needed the simplicity. Some things had been in my family for generations. In fact, it was a great concern to my mother that I didn't produce an offspring for things to be passed on to." Em stopped, then looked up at Sara. "Mothers often have expectations of one kind or another." She cradled her teacup again. "I really fulfilled many of my mother's expectations; I went to college, became a librarian, traveled, was somewhat of a career woman in my time. My mother encouraged those things and enjoyed seeing me achieve them."

Em stopped again and looked at Sara. Sara was listening quietly, feeling the empathy between the two of them.

"But she was quite vocal about her desire for a grandchild," Em continued. "Interestingly, when I occasionally went out with a fellow, she never seemed particularly pleased. I think she would have been quite satisfied with an immaculate conception."

Both women smiled at the thought of the librarian showing up pregnant in the staid old family in this small town. "Another interesting thought: it was to be a girl. The possibility of a grandson was never even mentioned." Em stood up from the table and straightened herself as much as possible. She arranged her face in a rather prim but authoritarian look. *A granddaughter to carry on our line. That's what we need, Emily, a granddaughter to carry on our line.* With that, Em sat down again. "I'd like to have a dollar for every time my mother said that."

Em took a little more fruit on her plate. "At any rate, she asked me to promise, many times in her life, and even when she was dying, not to allow these things to be sold in one of those horrid auctions, as she called them, where people bid over everything you had, right down to your hot water bottle." She paused, as if hearing her mother again. "Of course, I agreed over and over, not thinking at the time that I was the one who would be stuck with these generations of accumulations."

Sara nodded, thinking of the freedom she had felt in getting rid of the excess when she moved into her apartment.

"I've lived in this house all my life, but suddenly, a few years ago, I began to feel crowded here. I know that sounds silly—one person in this large house—but I felt like I needed more space. In fact, I felt it so strongly that I actually looked at the old Stronger home when it was for sale. That was about ten years ago, perhaps you remember. At any rate, you know which house I mean. Huge."

Sara nodded.

"In fact, I went so far as to make an offer on it, but it wasn't accepted. Strange as it seems now, I really felt quite distraught about that for awhile, because I thought the larger house was the answer to my problem. Finally I decided I had been distraught long enough, and I would just let go of the whole thing and go on about my business."

Em looked at Sara again. "I know you are going to understand this: One day I was just sitting quietly, and it came to me very clearly—I didn't need a larger house. What I needed was to get rid of things. All of the old things were too much of a burden for me. I wanted to clean out and make life simpler. And at the same moment I realized that, I knew just how to do it. Not by having an auction, but by selling things, a piece or two at a time, clearing just a little at a time. I could hardly wait to place the first ad in the paper."

Em stopped to take a bite of fruit and looked at Sara to see if she should continue, but Sara was looking at her intently and with understanding, so she went on. "The first thing to go was the piano. I was always bored to death by practicing, and preferred to listen to my records and hear people with some talent perform."

Em's face glowed as she told Sara about the young couple who bought the piano for their daughter. "But they didn't want the stool, because they had one that was in the family." Both women laughed at the irony of that.

"I learned something wonderful when I sold that piano," Em said. "It's not really about getting rid of things; it's more like recirculating them. I really enjoy seeing how happy other people are to take on the things I want to part with. It all depends on where you are in life. The trick is to know when to let go of something— when it is no longer useful to you, when it is more of a burden than a pleasure or even a perceived necessity."

"I guess I did much the same thing," Sara said, speaking for the first time in a long time. "Only I left mine all behind at once."

"Just another way to accomplish it," Em concluded.

Both women sat quietly for a few moments, their attention drawn to a robin working with twigs just outside the kitchen window.

"I appreciated your calling to check on me this past week," Sara said.

"Well, I am concerned that I may be telling you more than you want to know," Em said, looking at Sara questioningly.

"No," Sara said firmly. "I have rooms I need to clear out, too. No longer in my house, but in my mind, and I need your help to do it. The divorce is over with, the downsizing is complete, and the job has been terminated. It seems like the cleaning out has been done. I feel emptied, if you know what I mean, but now I am also stuck, just stuck here, not able to move forward with my life. I don't know how to go on." Sara stopped and looked across the table at the woman on the other side. "I guess I'm hoping that what you can tell me about the women who came before me will jar me loose, will help me find a sense of direction. I want you to tell me all of the rest of it. I want to know the rest of what happened between Matt and Annie. I want to know, Em. I have been studying the picture you gave me of Annie and an old photo I had of Jenn. I need to know the rest of the story."

Em sat quietly for awhile, looking out the window, then she turned back toward Sara and began speaking. "That summer, so many things happened that caused me to wonder. But of course I was just a girl myself and didn't fully understand as I do now, looking back. I told you that Matt and I were beginning to take an interest in boys, particularly one boy, the one with the car. Now I knew Matt had her cap set for him, so I understood that I could only play second fiddle or kind of go along for the ride, so to speak." Em looked at Sara to see if she understood, and when Sara nodded, Em continued. "I already knew enough not to cross Matt or interfere with her plans in any way, and that was okay with me because I mostly wanted to observe anyway, to see how this boyfriend business went. Unfortunately, I didn't foresee the outcome of things until it was too late."

§   §   §

Matt was laying out the plan.

"We'll go into Rochester for the street movie on Friday night, and we'll put our blanket on the back row just where they start to park the cars. That way we'll be sure to have a space back there. Then we'll go to the drugstore to get our drinks. We'll stay in there until he comes in, and that way we'll know he's there and has his car parked. Then we'll go out and move the blanket in front of his car while he's in there." Matt knew the boy's Free Movie Night habits, and had taken them all into consideration in her plan.

"After a while, I will act like I'm tired of sitting on the ground, and I'll get up and sit on his bumper," Matt continued. "You can say something to me like, 'You better not sit on that bumper. You could mess up the shine.' Then we'll see if he says anything to that. If not, we'll talk about it some more. We'll have to get his attention somehow. You follow my lead. I want to get him to ask me to sit in that car with him."

Em made a mental note to ask Matt for help if she ever wanted to get a particular boy to notice her.

"But he'll probably have his friend in the car with him," Annie put in.

"Yes, but in that case, he can get out and sit on the blanket with you."

Em began to feel a little uneasy, because she hadn't counted on having to do anything but watch. "I don't know," Em started out, "I don't know that other boy. I wouldn't know what to say—"

"It doesn't matter what you say," Matt broke in impatiently. "Don't say anything if you don't want to. Just sit there and watch the movie."

And so it was that by the next Friday evening, Matt had talked Harve into taking the three girls to Rochester to watch the street movie sponsored by the merchants in the little town. In the beginning, things went exactly according to Matt's plan. The girls arrived early and placed their blanket near the line where the cars would be expected to park, then went back into the drugstore to get their drinks and wait for the arrival of the boy.

On this warm summer evening, Matt had forsaken her jodhpurs and put on a dress. The dress made it obvious that she was well-developed for her age, and she had arranged the sash to assure that her new attributes wouldn't be missed. Em noticed that Matt hadn't added the sash until after Harve was out of sight.

"Here they come, and his friend is with him," Matt said, nodding toward the door. But the next move took the girls by surprise. The two boys walked straight toward them.

"Hi," said the tall one with the car. "Are you going to stay for the show?"

Being spoken to took Matt by surprise, but she recovered quickly. "I don't know," she hedged. "Is it supposed to be a good one tonight?"

"Western. Should be some good Indian fights. I don't remember the name of it, but they had it over in Kewanna last weekend. My friend here saw it over there and said it was good." His friend nodded.

"Well, in that case, maybe we will," Matt replied. "I guess I'll need to ring home and ask." With that, she started herding Em and Annie toward the front of the store where the telephone was located. "Maybe we'll see you later if it works out," she added.

"He's interested," Matt chortled to Em in a whisper. "Did you see how he walked right up and spoke to me? I didn't know he even knew who I was!" The excitement was evident in her voice as she continued. "You will have to go get that blanket and move it over by their car while I pretend I'm using the telephone. But don't stand by it, because I don't want him to know I put it there on purpose." Matt was busy positioning herself by the telephone so that no one could tell she wasn't actually ringing. "Hurry up," she added crossly. "Hurry up. And remember: don't stand by it. Come back in front of the store."

Em and Annie hurried off to gather up the blanket and put it in the designated spot, directly in front of the shiny black Chevy.

"I wonder where they will think we got a blanket if we didn't know we were going to stay for the show," Annie ventured to Em.

"I guess we can say we borrowed it," Em said rather glumly. This wasn't quite the way she had pictured getting acquainted with boys. She didn't recall it happening this way in any of the books she had read.

Matt was standing outside the store talking to the boys when

Em and Annie returned.

"It's okay if we stay. Harve said he would come back to pick us up at nine." Matt always called her father Harve, and Em never seemed to get used to it.

"I borrowed a blanket for us, just in case," Em said, deciding to bail out Matt this time.

"Oh, I'm really glad you thought of that," Matt said pointedly. Em couldn't tell if she was being sarcastic or if she was angry at being caught in a mistake.

As Matt led the three girls and two boys directly to the blanket in front of the shiny black Chevy, it occurred to Em to wonder how Matt would have known which blanket it was if Em had just borrowed it, but she decided to let that detail pass, and no one else seemed to notice. As for Matt, she was quite busy engaging the boy with the car.

"Is this car yours?" Matt was asking. "I really like that shiny black. My horse is black. That's probably the closest I'll ever get to having some shiny black transportation," she added pityingly. Em had never heard Matt being coy before.

"Well, girls don't need cars much anyway. Usually, your father takes you where you want to go until you get married, then your old man does. My mother doesn't even know how to drive," the tall boy concluded.

Em came up for air on that one. All of the women in her family had always driven, and she knew the women in Matt's family did too. She waited to see what Matt would say.

"Well, mechanical things are just too confusing for us girls, I guess, but we do love to see a nice, shiny car."

The movie had started, and people were beginning to indicate that they wanted the little group to sit down and be quiet, so the three girls arranged themselves on the blanket, and the boys climbed into the front seat of the much-admired Chevy parked right behind the blanket to watch the show.

"Lucky for me, Westerns have a love story in them or I wouldn't last," Em whispered to Annie as they arranged themselves for the twentieth time, trying to get comfortable on the hard street pavement. "I can only handle so much of people getting knocked off horses and getting hit in the back with hatchets."

Matt glanced at the girls and then leaned over toward Em. "Get ready," she whispered. "I'm going to make my move at the intermission. When we come back with our drinks, I will complain about my behind being sore from sitting on this street, and I will sit on the bumper of the car. You know what to do from there."

The Friday evening Free Street Movies had lengthy intermissions, ostensibly to give the projectionist time to set up the next reel of the film, but more likely to give the crowd plenty of time to patronize the sponsoring merchants. Everyone took great advantage of the time to buy sodas and candy and to visit with friends.

The two boys stayed at a distance from the girls during the intermission, and made a point to clown around with some other boys at the far end of the street, though Matt observed the tall boy looking in the girls' direction every now and then.

"Do you see how he keeps looking down here?" Matt questioned Em. "He really has noticed me. I can just tell. I'll get to ride in that car yet, just you wait and see."

Matt didn't spend any time during the intermission talking to the other young people at the movie, and when Em and Annie moved to join another group, Matt was adamant. "You stay here with me," Matt admonished both girls firmly. "If you go over there, you might not be here when I need you, and it will mess up the whole thing. Just stay right here," she added crossly. "It isn't going to kill you to do it this way once."

Em was beginning to wish she had never agreed to this whole thing, but it was not likely Matt would have taken "No" for an answer. She looked toward the car and noticed that the two boys had moved back over there and were standing outside, talking quietly and sometimes looking in the direction of the girls.

"See," Matt chimed, "you can see it too, can't you? He just keeps looking down here at me. I told you he noticed me." With that, she edged behind Em a little in order to adjust her sash. "Let's get over there; the movie's about to start. Remember what to do, and don't mess it up," Matt directed tersely.

The three girls headed toward the blanket, and Em noticed that the boys remained standing rather awkwardly by the car.

"I just don't see how I can stand to sit on this street again," Matt said rather loudly. "My rear end has totally gone dead from sitting on that hard pavement."

She paused to see if she was having any effect. There was no doubt the boys heard, because they were standing close enough, but neither of them made a move to reply.

"I suppose I could ring Harve to come get us early," Matt went on, trying a different track, "but I do hate to when this is such a good movie." Em noticed that Matt drew out the words *early* and *good* for a better effect. Matt had turned to look very plainly at Em now, and she pulled her skirt around her and sat right down on the front bumper of the shiny black Chevy.

"Oh! You'd better not sit on that," Em said, like she really meant it. "You might spoil the shine."

"Well, I simply can't sit on that hard street any longer, and I'm not going to miss the end of this movie," Matt said petulantly and loudly. Em began to worry that this was not going to work out the way Matt wanted, and she had noticed the tall boy saying something to his friend during Matt's performance. Just when Em was ready to give up and endure Matt's wrath for the rest of the evening, the tall boy spoke up.

"We were thinking, why don't you all sit in the car with us? There's plenty of room for five. I've had a lot more than that in here." By his tone, Em couldn't tell if he was more interested in inviting the girls or bragging about the car, but whichever, she was relieved that Matt's plan was working.

"Well-l-l-l, I don't know," Matt replied, then looked at Em. "Do you think it's okay?"

"I guess it would be all right, and it sure would be better than sitting on that hard street," Em said, trying to gain points with Matt and yet being careful not to draw attention to herself.

"Okay, that's settled," the tall boy said. Then he turned to look directly at Annie. "You're kind of short, so why don't you get in the front with me, and then you can see better." He was obviously pleased with himself. "The rest of you can get in the back seat. There's plenty of room." He took a peek at Annie again to see her reaction, and when she said nothing, he continued. "Well, let's hop in, the thing's about ready to start." There was no mistaking the look on his face or the excitement in his voice.

Em stood still as a stone. In fact, her body felt as if it had turned to stone. She felt as if nothing in the world could make her move, but somehow she was getting into the automobile, sandwiching in between Matt and the other boy. She felt as if her body didn't belong to her, as if she were just watching the whole scene from somewhere else. She sat stock still, waiting for the reaction from Matt. Matt was sitting stiffly beside her and was silent.

Em remembered nothing of the rest of the evening, nothing of the movie or getting back out of the car or moving to the corner by the drugstore to wait for Harve to pick them up. She didn't recall if anything was said by anyone. She was only conscious that Matt was absolutely quiet.

"Well, was the show worth all that long, hard sit?" Harve asked.

Em's mind registered that someone needed to reply, so she made the attempt. "It was pretty good," she started out, also becoming aware that Matt still had the sash on. "Too many Indian fights for me though." She wished Matt would at least say something.

The ride home seemed to take forever, and neither Matt nor Annie said one word, so Em tried to keep up with Harve's comments while her mind was occupied with what she would do when the two girls were at home alone. She knew that Matt would not let this pass.

Jenn was sitting at the kitchen table reading when the girls came in, and she began to ask her usual questions: "Did you have a good time?" "How was the show?" "Did you see any of your friends?"

Em answered for the three of them, because Matt had simply walked stiffly through the room and gone upstairs without saying a word. Annie stood quietly, not saying anything, waiting to go upstairs when Em did.

Matt was already lying in bed with her eyes closed when Em and Annie got to the bedroom. Em thought it over and decided not to say anything. Annie undressed silently, pulled on her gown, and climbed into bed, turning her back to Matt as she usually did. Em carefully climbed into bed, lying down next to Matt's stiff body; she tried to close her eyes, but she felt as if she were waiting, just waiting and waiting, and it was getting to be dawn when she finally went to sleep.

THE RIDE

*E*m was on the third floor, sitting alone in the tower, when she saw the black car coming down the road toward the house. She got up from her perch and stood very still, staring out the half-hexagon windows at the car, hoping it would pass. As she continued to watch, she realized the car was slowing to turn in the lane and that it really was the shiny black Chevy from the night before, that the tall boy was driving and his friend was in the passenger seat.

Matt had not spoken to Em or to Annie since the night before, and Em noticed that Annie was careful to avoid being alone with Matt and was spending most of her time helping Jenn. Em watched from the tower window as Harve approached the car when it pulled to the front of the house. She couldn't hear the conversation between the two, the man and the boy, but she saw the boy get out of the car and lean against it, talking to the man in a comfortable fashion. In a few moments, Harve and the boy walked around the car, evidently admiring it, and then they raised the hood of the automobile.

"Maybe he has a problem and he's come to ask Harve about it," Em said to herself hopefully. She watched the two people carefully, looking for signs to tell her what was being said between them. The man and the boy talked for what seemed to Em to be an interminable length of time, and the friend finally got out of the car to join them. There was a handshake between Harve and the friend, so Em assumed Harve was acquainted already with the tall boy in some way, but was just now meeting his friend.

Quite a bit more conversation occurred among the three of them, with much gesturing and looking under the hood of the car. Just as Em was beginning to become more comfortable with the visit, the tall boy slammed shut the hood of the Chevy and all three people—Harve, with the two boys alongside—headed for the back door of the house. Em walked as quietly as she could to the stair door on the third floor and opened it, hoping to catch some of the conversation that would be coming up from the kitchen.

"Jenn!" Harve called in from the back door. "Jenn! We have some company here." This was followed by much stomping as the three cleared their boots to come into the kitchen. "Thought maybe you could set a couple of extra plates since it's right at dinner time."

Jenn answered in the affirmative and immediately sent Annie to the smokehouse to get some more ham. Em could hear her pulling jars of jelly, pickles, and beets from the cupboard. Jenn knew how to stretch a meal; her mother had taught her that. Em could hear her mixing a second batch of cornbread, sticking it in the oven, and then rearranging the plates on the table while Harve and the boys discussed the merits of the new Chevy's engine.

Em understood that it would just be a matter of minutes until all of them would be seated around the table, and just as she was thinking it, Jenn called up the stairway to her. "Em! Can you come down here? We have company for dinner and I need your help." Reluctantly, Em headed down the stairs.

Jenn was bustling. "Can you go out and find Matt? Tell her we have company for dinner. On her way in, have her go to the cellar and bring up a can of apples. And you go to the smokehouse to help Annie finish getting the ham. She may have trouble reaching it and it's pretty heavy for her to lift down."

Em hurried out the kitchen door, relieved that Harve and the boys were busy in conversation and didn't take time to say anything to her. She found Matt coming toward the house from the apple grove.

"We have company for dinner," Em said. She waited carefully for the reply as she knew Matt couldn't have missed seeing the shiny black Chevy in the drive. There was no reply. "Jenn wants you to bring up a can of apples from the cellar." Still nothing. "Better this cellar than the one on the farm with that awful door," Em continued, trying to lighten things up a bit, but actually only addressing Matt's back as she continued to walk toward the house without saying a word.

Em went on to the smokehouse to help Annie as directed, but Annie was finished and was already walking toward the house with the ham. There was nothing left to do but go into the house and sit down at the table for dinner.

"I remember when your dad got his car," Harve was saying to the tall boy. "He was the first one around to have one. We were all jealous. Seems odd he has a boy old enough to drive now. Time sure flies." Harve was reaching for the potatoes. He always served himself first.

"Jenn, the boys were telling me they met Matt and Annie and Em last evening at the street movie. So I really don't know if this visit is to show me that new car or to call on these young ladies." Harve was talking in his artificial tone of voice again, and his comment made both the boys and girls uncomfortable, so for awhile nothing was said as Harve picked up the dishes one at a time, helped himself, and then passed them on.

It was Jenn who finally broke the silence, curious too about what this visit was to mean. "The girls liked the movie," Jenn ventured. "What did you boys think of it?"

"I thought it was good, myself," the tall boy replied, "and he must have liked it," he added, indicating his friend, "because he's seen it twice."

Jenn shook her head in agreement, and the tall boy continued. "Long one though—three reels. I invited the girls to sit in my car. I hope that was okay. That street gets pretty hard. I sure do remember that from before I had my car." He was talking fast now instead of eating, as if trying to get everything said he had come to say. "I hope you didn't mind that I asked them." He glanced at Annie now and his face colored. Harve took a sharp look at Matt, who was looking at her plate, and then at the tall boy. He caught the glance at Annie and the coloring of the boy's face.

"Not at all," Harve responded heartily. "Nice of you to do it. Not every day you get to sit in a nice new Chevy, right girls?" When no one responded, Harve continued, "That car is so new it still smells new. Now I don't want you smoking in that thing, son, and smelling it all up."

"No sir, I don't smoke," the tall boy said, pleased to be making a good impression on Harve. He cleared his throat and fidgeted in his chair, obviously getting ready for the next thing he had to say. "The girls said you have horses out at the farm," he started out with a little crack in his voice. "So I was wondering if we all might be able to go out to ride sometime. Dad sold ours, and I miss getting to ride. I was getting pretty good at it, and I miss it. I could help the girls if they need it."

He was talking fast again, making sure to get the point about his capability in with Harve, and making sure Harve understood he was asking the girls to go, too. He reached across the table and stuck his fork in a pickle and transferred it to his plate just as he had seen Harve do a few minutes earlier. "We can all go out in the car. That way you won't have to make a trip," the tall boy continued.

Em thought that the boy must have been awake all night figuring this out. She looked at the tall boy then looked at Harve, waiting for his reply. Harve didn't say anything but busied himself with his pickled beet slices, arranging them so he could stab a neat stack of them with his fork. Everyone else was silent, concentrating intensely on eating.

Finally, Harve had the beets corralled and he looked at the tall boy. "Well now," he began, "that's nice of you to offer. The girls like to ride, but I don't get out there as often as I should to take them." He added an explanation. "What with the hired man taking care of the farm and all, right now."

It was obvious that the tall boy didn't understand the special living arrangement, but it was just as obvious that he had accomplished what he came for, so it didn't matter. Em winced at the thought of going riding. Though she had often ridden, it wasn't something she especially enjoyed, and she knew Annie was actually afraid of the horses. Matt was the only one who liked to ride and was good at it. She looked at Matt, but she appeared to be busy with her food, seeming not to be concerned one way or another with this conversation.

"How about if we go after dinner then," the tall boy ventured. "We can go home and change into some riding clothes." He stopped to indicate his friend. "And we'll be back here in no time."

He definitely had been up all night planning this, Em thought.

"I reckon that would do just fine," Harve replied, and the matter was settled.

Em could barely swallow the rest of her dinner; Matt was pushing hers around on her plate; and Annie had stopped eating altogether. The boys shoveled in the last few bites on their plates and got up to leave, evidently finished with what they came to do and anxious to get home to change into their riding clothes.

As soon as the boys and Harve had moved out front to take one last look at the black Chevy, Matt went out through the back door and headed again toward the apple grove.

"I don't know what gets into that girl sometimes," Jenn commented. "She's barely said a word all day. Not even a surly one."

Em pushed the plate scraps into the slop pail, and Annie put the leftover pickles and beets back into the jars.

"Nice of the boys to ask to take you out to ride," Jenn said, fishing for some comments from the girls. "I thought I noticed the tall one looking at you." She directed this comment to Annie. Annie's face colored, but she didn't reply. "What did you think about that, Em? Did you notice him looking at Annie?"

"I don't know," Em hedged. "I guess I wasn't paying attention." She hoped Jenn would let the matter drop.

"Tell you what," Jenn continued, giving up for the time being, "I'll take care of these dishes today. You girls go and get ready. They'll be back for you pretty soon."

The girls turned to go, and Jenn pulled Annie aside. "I know you're not too good with the horses," she said. "Let the boy help you if you need it." With that she laughed and winked and gave Annie a flick on her rear with the dishtowel to send her on her way.

"I really don't like to ride," Annie said plainly as she and Em slipped on their dungarees and boots.

"Well, it isn't my favorite way to spend an afternoon either, but

I think you are the one who's really being asked to go riding," Em said. She wanted to see if Annie was aware the boy was interested in her.

Annie stopped in the midst of pulling on her boots and looked directly at Em. Her face was full of distress. "I know," she replied.

"What do you think," Em pursued. "Do you think he's nice? Do you like him?"

"You know that's not the point," Annie said as she turned to head back toward the kitchen.

The two girls sat on the back steps, making small talk while they waited for the black Chevy to come back down the road. Matt was nowhere to be seen, and Em wondered if she would show up in time to go riding. Just as Em thought that Matt had definitely decided not to go, she saw the car coming down the road, and Matt appeared, seemingly ready to go. She had evidently been watching for the car and timed her arrival at the steps just as the boys came up the drive. Matt still said nothing as the three girls climbed into the back seat of the Chevy. The two boys sat in the front.

I'm grateful for the seating arrangement, Em thought as they headed off down the road. But it didn't take long for her to figure out that the seating arrangement wouldn't make any difference. Matt still didn't add one word to the conversation.

As soon as they arrived at the farm house, the hired hand and his son came out of the house to admire the new Chevy. Just like Harve, they seemed content to spend considerable time checking out the engine.

"I'm going on down to the barn to get the tack and saddle up," Matt spoke up to Em, startling her.

"Okay," Em replied, taken aback by the first words Matt had uttered since the night before and also relieved that Matt hadn't asked for her help. She was none too fond of working with horses. "We'll be down in a few minutes," she called after Matt, hoping to sound like everything was back to normal.

Em and Annie continued to stand around rather awkwardly until the man and boys finally finished their appraisal of the new Chevy and slammed the hood down.

"Okay to leave her parked right here while we go riding?" the tall boy asked.

"Sure thing. Maybe someone will think she's mine."

With that, the two boys and Em and Annie took off for the barn. Matt had all five horses saddled and bridled when the others arrived.

"Hey, these are good-looking horses!" the tall boy exclaimed. "Every bit as good as you said." The two boys were walking around the hitching rail, looking over each horse in turn, admiringly. "I know the black one's yours," he said to Matt. "Would it be okay if I ride this Chestnut? She sure is a beautiful filly." He was running his hand along the horse's auburn coat and stroking her pale cream mane.

"Sure," Matt replied. "She'll be a good one for you. That's the one I would have picked for you. She's got high spirits, but I heard you say you were good, so I know you can handle her."

Em was glad to see that Matt was getting into the spirit of things, and she was also glad she didn't draw the Chestnut to ride. She was a beautiful horse, no doubt about it, but she hadn't been broken long and didn't really care that much about carrying riders. When Em had seen others ride her, she noticed it took a strong rein and good control to keep her from heading back to the barn.

The tall boy's friend chose the spotted horse, probably for its cowboy appeal. Em then climbed on the Bay, expecting that Annie would ride the docile dapple gray and Matt would ride Nightmare. Em was just turning to follow the boys away from the rail when she saw Matt mounting the gray. Annie looked bewildered.

"You take Nightmare," Matt was saying. "I want you to have the best horse today."

"I don't want to," Annie protested. "He's only used to you. Anyway, he's your horse."

Em saw the frightened look on Annie's face. "Matt, I don't think she's strong enough to handle that horse. She's never ridden him before, and he's only used to you. You know he takes a strong hand. I've seen how you have to work with him. It takes a good rider." Em was talking fast, almost pleading now.

"Nonsense. I've got him trained. Quit being such a baby and get on." She directed this last at Annie as she moved the dapple gray in closer. "Here, I've got the rein for you. And hurry up. They're going to wonder what happened to us."

Annie took a quick, distressed look at Em and climbed into the saddle on Nightmare's back.

"After all," Matt was saying in a mocking voice, "if you're old enough to have a boyfriend, you're old enough to take on a spirited horse."

The boys were already out front, walking their horses through the pasture behind the back barn lot. Em noticed that the tall boy was having to work to keep the Chestnut filly from turning back to the barn. She was shaking her head and prancing sideways. The tall boy was using his heels and the reins to keep firm control of the filly when she acted up. Em was relieved to see that he seemed to be enjoying the challenge and was able to counter the horse's every move. He was an accomplished horse person, Em decided. She was relieved, because she was uncertain about Matt's motive in giving the tall boy the troublesome filly to ride. Her other concern was Annie, and she turned to look back to see how she was doing with Nightmare. The horse seemed to be behaving himself and, in fact, was walking along as docilely as Em had ever seen him, perhaps in awe of the strange rider on his back.

"When I teach this girl who's boss, we'll cut loose a little," the tall boy called to the girls. "Just give me a while with a walk and a trot so I can get a feel for handling her."

Em was more than glad to hear that and would certainly be content to walk and trot throughout the whole ride. She dropped back to walk her horse beside Annie's. "Okay with me to walk until we're finished," she said quietly. Annie nodded in agreement, and Em noticed she was starting to look a little more comfortable on Nightmare's back.

The girls continued to walk their horses slowly, giving the boys plenty of space to work with the horses they were not used to riding. Nightmare began to get a little impatient with this as he was used to leading in a ride. In fact, he was not used to being in a ride with the Chestnut filly, as Matt was the only person who usually rode that horse, too. The Chestnut was actually Harve's horse, picked for her looks, and he broke her himself, though she had not been broken long. Em thought that Harve had probably not ridden her this summer. Her thoughts about the Chestnut were interrupted by snorting from the horse next to her and she turned to see the distressed look on Annie's face.

"He's getting impatient," Annie called out to Matt. "I don't know if I can keep him back." She looked toward Em again and Em saw the panic in her eyes. Nightmare was pulling ahead of Em's horse, breaking from a walk into a trot. Matt was lagging back on the dapple gray, and Em wondered briefly why she didn't pull forward to be in position in case Annie needed help. Her question was quickly answered.

"Let's just go then!" Matt yelled. "Git up horse!"

At the sound of Matt's voice, Nightmare broke into a gallop, bent on taking the lead from the Chestnut filly. Riding just behind Nightmare, her own horse now in a gallop, Em knew that Annie would be no match for Nightmare when he was excited.

Just as she was trying to think what she might be able to do to calm the horse, Em thought she noticed a barely perceptible slip in Nightmare's saddle. At the same time, the black horse quickened his pace, passed the Chestnut filly, and headed toward the barbed-wire fence at the long pasture's edge.

"He's going to try to take her off!" the tall boy yelled back toward the others. He worked quickly to move the Chestnut filly over toward Nightmare which only seemed to aggravate the black horse further. At the same time, Nightmare edged toward the fence with the filly close beside, Em again saw the saddle slip in the direction Annie was leaning, and she watched in disbelief as Annie was scraped along the barbed wire and thrown over the fence into the other pasture. The tall boy reined his horse up tight and was off and over the fence in a split second, leaving Nightmare and the Chestnut filly to gallop away, vying for the lead.

"We need some help! She's hurt real bad! She's bleeding!" The boy was screaming toward Matt now, and Matt turned the dapple gray back toward the house.

Em was off her horse and climbing over the fence now, just catching the fear in Annie's eyes before she closed them and began moaning then alternately grimacing and vomiting.

"Her arm's broke. That's for sure. Just look at it," the tall boy was yelling, even though Em was right beside him and Matt had gone to the house for help and the other boy was rounding up the horses. Em looked toward Annie's bent forearm and saw the bone sticking through. At the same time, she tried to turn Annie's head to the side so she wouldn't choke as she retched. For a moment, Em felt lightheaded and wondered if she could do this. The tall boy was looking at Annie's lower leg where blood was beginning to seep through a long gash in her dungarees.

"I'm going to have to tie this up," he said, still yelling, and at the same time pulling off his shirt. "I need to get this bleeding stopped here." He quieted his voice just a little. While he worked to pull up the leg of Annie's dungarees and position his shirt around the long gash, Em noticed that Annie was literally covered with gashes of all sizes from the barbed wire fence and that they were all bleeding. The wound on her leg seemed to be by far the worst, though, so she began to feel some confidence in the tall boy's judgment.

Just as Annie began retching again, the hired man pulled up to the barbed-wire fence in his truck, with Matt in the seat beside him and his son in the back end.

"My wife's ringing the Doc and her folks," the man said, scrambling over the fence. "Don't you worry now, little lady," he was saying to Annie, "we'll have you fixed up in no time." Em saw him take a quick look at the bone sticking out Annie's arm and the widening spot of blood seeping through the shirt tied around her leg, and she noticed his face start to pale. "We've got to get you into the truck," he was saying. "You just hang on now, little lady."

"No," the tall boy countered. Em was surprised at how mature he looked. "She can't ride in the back of the truck. Too hard on her." He was pulling keys from his pocket. "Go and get the Chevy."

Em vowed that the tall boy would always be her friend.

Matt went again with the hired man and his son, and Em was left to comfort Annie as best she could while the boy looked for ways to stop the bleeding in as many places as possible.

Annie continued retching and moaning, and it seemed an interminable time before the hired man pulled up in the shiny black car with his son and Matt following closely in the pickup truck.

"Doc's on his way and so's your folks, little lady," he said as he motioned for the boys to get ready to lift Annie into the back of the Chevy. There was no doubt he thought they ought not waste any time.

"Em," Annie said, grimacing as they placed her on the seat.

"Get back there with her," the tall boy said as he got in the driver's side.

Em had a strange moment of awareness of all the blood on the seats of the shiny new black car, then she turned her attention again to Annie, telling her everything would be okay. Annie had stopped retching and was just sobbing softly.

Doc Whitney was just pulling into the drive as the Chevy and old pickup pulled through the back barn-lot gate into the yard. He was out of his vehicle, bag in hand.

"Just leave her right there," he said when the boys opened the door and he saw the blood. "No need to move her any more just now. I can examine her right there. She's been moved enough." Doc always sounded most gruff and official when he was most concerned, Em thought. He started immediately cutting the dungarees and the blood-soaked shirt off her leg.

"That's a deep one, but looks like no major vessels are cut," he said, still in his official voice. "We can just clean that out and sew it shut, bandage her up real tight, and in a while you'll be good as new," he assured Annie. "In the meantime, I can give you something here to help you rest for awhile." He had pulled a syringe from his bag and filled it, injecting it just as Harve and Jenn pulled into the back lot.

"What happened here?" Harve was running toward the black Chevy, Jenn close behind.

"Horse threw her over the barbed-wire fence," the tall boy said.

Harve had Doc by the arm, turning Doc toward him. "Is she hurt bad? How bad is it?"

Jenn knelt by Annie's head, touching her hair gently, not knowing where else was safe to touch.

"Well," Doc said, "I'd say this girl got lucky again. We've got a real bad gash on her leg, but no major vessel cut, and the boy tied it up with his shirt and kept the bleeding down." Doc seemed to be speaking in his regular voice, now that the worst of the crisis was past, and he nodded toward the tall boy. The boy blushed, suddenly aware that he was standing in front of the whole group half naked. He immediately went around to the trunk of the Chevy and pulled out a blanket to put around his shoulders. Doc turned his attention back to Harve and Jenn.

"I just gave her a pretty stiff shot of morphine, so she should be out of pain here in a few minutes," Doc explained. "I think the best thing is to take her home for now, and you can clean her up the best you can while she's out." He was looking at Jenn. "Then I'll come first thing in the morning and set the arm."

He turned around to address Harve. "It's a bad break. I'll probably have to give her a little ether to get it done. You have the kitchen table ready." He looked at Jenn again. "Soon as the morphine takes hold here, I'll clean that leg gash and bandage it up real tight, then I can wait till morning to suture it when I've got her under. She's had enough for today."

Annie's body had relaxed and she began breathing deeply and regularly. Doc gently worked on the gash in her leg while Jenn sat scrunched on the floor of the back seat of the Chevy, lightly stroking her daughter's hair and telling her softly that she was there with her and that she would be all right.

When Doc finished dressing the wound on Annie's leg, he turned to the tall boy. "Can you just take her on home, son?" he asked. "I hate to move her any more than necessary, especially since she seems to be resting okay."

The boy nodded and again climbed in the driver's seat. "You just stay right there, Ma'am," he said, turning with gentleness to Jenn. "I'll take it real slow and try not to disturb her any."

Harve had stepped to the side of the car and put his hand on the boy's blanketed shoulder. "I'll help you with this car, son," he said, looking at the inside of the Chevy.

Matt climbed into the car with her father, and so did the tall boy's friend. This left Em to ride home in the front seat of the Chevy, so she climbed in.

"He faints pretty easy," the tall boy said to Em by way of explanation for his friend's distance during the whole ordeal.

"I see," Em said, for lack of anything better.

Neither one spoke again, but sat quietly, listening to the slow hum of the motor and the soft words of the mother comforting her daughter in the back seat of the car.

"I never knew that dapple gray to throw anyone," Jenn said finally. "You usually can't get that horse to even break out of a trot."

THE BRICK HOUSE

*E*m passed the night fitfully. She was aware of Matt's curled body, back toward her, on the opposite side of the bed. She thought, sometimes, from the sound of her breathing, that Matt was asleep, but she couldn't be sure. She thought about saying something to Matt about what had happened that afternoon, about any part of it, but she didn't know where to start, and Matt hadn't said a word to her, so she had to assume that Matt didn't want to talk about it.

Em was unused to having something like this happen in the family, and no one talking about it. It was as though, if no one spoke about it, it would be erased. In fact, several times as Em was about to doze off, she would awaken abruptly and wonder if the accident really did happen, if Annie really was lying on the couch drugged and hurt. Once, she considered going to the other room to look, to see if Annie was there, to see if it was really true. Then she looked at Matt's back and she knew that it had happened; and she cried.

She cried because she missed her mother. She wanted to talk to her mother about this. In her family, she and her mother would talk about this. They would go over every detail of the day, talk until they couldn't think of anything else to say, and then they'd say the same things all over again. They would talk until their bodies and minds began to calm down.

"Let's get this out of our system," her mother would say. "Let's just talk about this and get it out of our system."

Em wished now that she had some way to get this out of her

system. She wished she had not seen the slight slip of the saddle. Perhaps she had not, she reasoned. Perhaps she had imagined that. What if her mother were here now? What would she say about that? Would she tell her mother what she thought she saw? Would she say Matt had insisted that Annie ride Nightmare? Why didn't she tell Jenn that Annie was riding the black horse and not the dapple gray as Jenn presumed? Did anyone tell Jenn that? Em wondered about all these things as she turned again to look at Matt's back.

It was in the purple-gray light of predawn when Em began to hear noises coming from the direction of the kitchen, and she knew Jenn and Harve must be getting ready for Doc Whitney. Unable to stay in bed with her own thoughts any longer, she climbed out of bed and pulled on the dungarees and shirt she had worn the day before. Checking them over, she discovered the side of her pants leg was stiff with dried blood and quickly pulled them off again, acutely aware of her answer to the question about the realness of what had happened. She took a last look at Matt's back curled up on the far side of the bed and headed out of the room.

Harve and Jenn had water boiling on the stove. They had covered the kitchen table with several layers of blankets and topped the whole thing off with a clean white sheet. Em caught the soft moans coming from the other room just as Doc Whitney came stomping in through the back door.

"Good set up," he said, looking at the table. His voice was gruff again, and he shifted his attention to the direction of the moans.

"The shot seemed to wear off about two o'clock," Jenn explained, "and she's been in a lot of pain since. I was wondering if you could give her another one now." She finished hurriedly.

"Can't because of the ether," Doc responded just as quickly, "but she won't be feeling anything here in just a few minutes. Won't take me a couple minutes to get ready to go." His voice was still gruff, but his eyes were tender toward Jenn.

"Coffee, if you need some," Harve said, cocking his head toward the stove.

"Pour me a cup to cool while I get this ether going, then make sure the fire is out. You and I are going to have to carry her in here." He was looking at Harve, gauging Harve's ability to handle the task of carrying his groaning, bloody daughter to the kitchen without passing out.

Harve took a slug of scalding coffee from his own cup and followed Doc toward the couch in the other room.

Em stood in the hallway door and looked at Jenn who stood with her back toward the room; she was looking out the window toward the breaking dawn. Em lowered her own eyes to the floor and the two stood, the woman and the girl, listening to the moans and cries and reassurances as Annie was carried into the room and placed on the kitchen table.

"Your mother will be right here with you," Doc said; he pointed out a place for Jenn to stand. Gratefully, Jenn moved forward and touched Annie's hair, taking her place beside her daughter.

"You won't feel a thing, and when you wake up we'll have you all put back together in fine shape," Doc said, addressing Annie in his stiff voice again. "Now off you go to dreamland." He finished speaking as he held the mask in place over her nose and mouth and began dripping the anesthetic onto it.

The heavy smell of ether began to drift around the room. Jenn's face turned pale, and she moved her feet a bit as if to make herself more stable. Harve leaned against the kitchen sink and took several more gulps of coffee. Em remembered the sinking, smothering ether feeling from when she had her tonsils out; she covered her nose and turned her head to get a breath of air from the hallway. For a split second, it crossed her mind that Matt still was not there.

Doc finally set the bottle down and corked it tightly. "I'll take a shot of that coffee now," he said, totally unaffected, "while I make sure this is doing the work."

Harve scrambled to get the cup, relieved to be distracted from the strong odor.

Doc took three long, slow draughts, evidently relishing the warmth and the strength the brew gave him.

"We'll tackle this arm first while she's out good," he said, just as if he were presenting for a new class of medical students. "This is a compound fracture, because it came through the skin, too. So we have to get the bone back in place and then take care of the external wound."

For a moment, Em felt strangely detached, like she was watching the teacher put a math equation on the board.

Doc Whitney pushed down hard on Annie's shoulder, braced his hip against the table, and gave a strong, sharp pull. The motion was so coordinated and so swift, Em hardly realized what was happening, but the minute it was over, she felt the queasiness rising in her stomach; she turned again toward the hallway to get a breath of air and to get her bearings.

Doc had his sutures and needle out now, preparing to sew up the outer wound on Annie's arm. "Good skin flap left here." He was addressing his class again. "Should get by without too much of a scar."

Em was surprised at how quickly and deftly he worked. She looked at Annie's arm and, except for the neat row of stitches, it really did look normal again.

"Bad as they may look, all these smaller scrapes and scratches will heal themselves with just a little help from you, Mother." He was looking at Jenn. "I'll leave some ointment for you and directions about applying it." As he said this last, he was examining several of the longer cuts, cleaning them, and passing on to the next area of wounds.

"This is the one we have to watch out for," he said, taking on his gruff tone again. He moved down toward Annie's leg and began to lay open the wound and work with it slowly and carefully— cleaning, probing, wiping away the now fresh blood. Em steadied herself against the doorway. "This will look good when I'm done with it." Doc's voice was softer now. "But the damage is very deep. A blood clot is possible with a wound like this."

He looked toward Jenn. "She will look pretty good when we're through here," he repeated emphatically, "but she will need to lie quietly for several days. The danger here is a blood clot." He looked at Jenn again to make sure she had heard him, to make sure she was registering what he was saying. "We're not completely out of the woods here yet."

Doc made a final tie on Annie's leg-wound sutures, made a deft move with the small scissors, then turned toward his coffee cup.

Em suddenly realized that she had been watching the whole procedure, and she felt her knees grow a little weak. She turned again to take a deep breath from the hallway and realized Matt, still in her nightclothes, was standing behind her.

"I didn't know you were up," Em said, startled. Without a word, Matt turned and headed back down the hall toward the bedroom.

"Let's just let her lie here awhile," Doc directed this toward Harve. "We'll finish our coffee, then I'll help you get her back in the other room before I leave." He took his cup and went toward Jenn's big rocker by the kitchen stove.

For a time, no one spoke. Harve poured himself another cup of coffee, freshened Doc's cup, and went back to lean against the sink. Jenn didn't move from her place near Annie's head, and Doc laid his head against the tall back of the rocker, raising it just enough to take a deep drink of the warm coffee periodically.

Em began to consider returning to the bedroom to see if she could find Matt when Doc spoke again. "I can't say strongly enough that she needs to be kept still for a few days," he started out, looking back and forth from Jenn to Harve. "The leg wound is serious. Deep. Lots of bleeding. There are two things to be concerned about." He was addressing Jenn now. "Clots, we can't see. That's out of our hands now. But you need to watch for redness around that wound, especially any streaks. That's a sign of infection, and I would need to know about that right away." Another long draught of coffee. "Another thing: she's going to be very uncomfortable for a few days. The arm will be painful and so will the leg wound, so I'm going to leave you some morphine and directions about how often she's to have it. If it gets too bad, I can come by and give her a shot, but I think the tablets will do the trick."

With these last words, Doc lifted himself out of Jenn's rocker, drained his coffee cup, and began to rummage around in his black leather bag. He held up a big tube of salve. "Twice a day on all the cuts and scrapes and wounds," he said to Jenn. "And this is the morphine." He poured several large, round, white pills from a large bottle into a smaller one. "No more than one every four hours, no matter what." He was holding the bottle up in front of him and shaking it slightly to emphasize his point. "This may begin to wear off before the time's up, but only one every four hours. I know you will be upset if you see her hurting, but no more often than every four hours. This is strong stuff."

Evidently satisfied that Jenn understood what he was saying, Doc walked over to the kitchen cupboard, opened the door, and set the bottle inside. "Keep this put up when you're not using it." He turned toward Harve. "Now let's get her situated in the other room while she's still under."

Jenn hurried ahead to adjust the sheets on the couch in the parlor as the two men carefully carried Annie down the hall toward the front room. Jenn continued to fuss over the bedding around Annie, as Harve walked Doc back down the hallway and through the kitchen to the back door.

"Thanks for everything," Harve said, shaking Doc's hand.

"I don't want to worry her mother more than necessary," Doc said nodding toward the front of the house. "You know how women are." He smiled. "But you need to help enforce her lying still. Some large blood vessels are damaged in that leg. That makes clotting a factor to be reckoned with. Keep her still with the morphine if you have to. But don't give her more than one every four hours. Her mother will probably want to give her one the first time she whimpers. You know how a woman can be about seeing one of her children in distress."

With this last, he smiled knowingly at Harve and patted him on the shoulder. The two men put on coats and headed out the back door toward Doc Whitney's car.

Em headed toward the parlor. "Can I help you fix things in here?" she asked Jenn.

"Yes, I can use some help," Jenn replied. "What I want to do while she's still under is just kind of make this into a sick room for awhile. I want to clear that side table and put it over here by the couch, and bring that rose chair over here, because someone will need to sit with her all the time for the next few days. We'll need to take turns." Jenn spoke as if she were talking to herself. "And we'll take those two straight chairs into the kitchen so that can be our sitting room for now. That way if she's resting, we won't bother her."

Em realized that Jenn was doing what she did best at such times—getting things organized. Except for the strong smell of ether in the room, the mother and the girl worked together to prepare the room much in the same way they worked to stretch the noon meal when unexpected company came the day before. This thought drew Em's mind back to the vision of the barely perceptible slip of the saddle on the black horse. Hurriedly, she picked up one of the straight chairs Jenn had designated and headed toward the kitchen, grateful for the distraction and grateful for some breaths of fresh air from the hallway.

At some point, it occurred to Em that Matt still was not there, but Jenn kept Em hopping with the rearrangements in the kitchen and the parlor, so she let that thought pass from her mind too.

Jenn tended to Annie all during that first day. She comforted her when she moaned, held her head over the wash basin while she retched with the after-effects of the ether, and gave her the morphine tablets, being very careful about the four-hour time lapse the doctor had mandated.

After the parlor and kitchen were arranged to her satisfaction, Jenn was quite preoccupied with Annie and seemed not to want any help, so Em went back to the bedroom to see about Matt. She was curious that Matt could keep herself so scarce through all this, yet she wasn't anxious to confront Matt because she wasn't sure what to say. Matt wasn't in the bedroom so she needn't have worried about it, though Em saw her nightshirt lying on the unmade bed; she assumed she had dressed and gone outside.

Since she didn't know what her place was in all this, Em decided to take a book up to the third floor tower in the old brick house and settle herself there for awhile. She situated herself in Annie's favorite place by the window overlooking the front drive. As soon as she sat down, her attention focused on the drive.

She envisioned yesterday, when the new black Chevy pulled up with the two boys in it. From there, her mind played through the events of the day—over and over again. Trying as hard as she could, she still could not concentrate on the story printed on the pages before her; she could only reflect on what had happened to Annie. She thought again about the black horse and the dapple gray as if to make sure she had that right in her mind, then she was on horseback again, looking ahead, looking at the black horse from behind, looking again to see if the saddle really did slip.

The slam of a car door in the drive finally brought her back to the present and she looked down into the yard to recognize the truck that belonged to the hired man from the farm. Harve was walking toward him as he and his son stepped out of the truck, and the three of them stood together and talked for awhile. The men and the boy didn't come toward the house, and in few minutes the hired man and his son got back in the truck and drove away. Harve headed back toward the house.

"Em? Em, are you up there?" It was Jenn's voice calling to her up the back stairway. "Will you come down, please? We all need to talk some things over here."

"Coming," Em replied. She stood up to go, but she was unsure her legs would carry her; they felt so heavy. Had the hired man told Harve that Annie was on the black horse? Or had he found that the saddle was loose? Not possible, Annie reasoned, because Harve hadn't had enough time to get into the house and convey all that to Jenn. Still, it seemed to take her forever to make her way down the twisting back stairs to the first floor and into the kitchen.

Em was surprised to see Matt already sitting at the kitchen table next to Harve. She wondered for a minute how Matt could have avoided her all day, where she could have been. But she realized she was relieved not to have seen her anyway, so she didn't say anything to Matt now. Matt didn't speak. Jenn was sitting in her rocker, so Em took a seat in one of the straight chairs she had brought in from the parlor earlier in the day.

"We need to make some plans here," Jenn said. Em could see that Jenn was ready to get a handle on things by doing some more organizing. "We need to decide who will sit with Annie when. I don't want her left by herself until she's out of the woods, as Doc says. I don't want her getting up for anything. There's the bedpan to tend to, and something for her to eat and drink when she feels up to it."

Em could tell Jenn was more comfortable having thought this out, and Em actually felt more comfortable too, knowing she would have something to do. As if reading her thoughts, Jenn turned to her. "I'm really glad you're here to help us with this, Em," she said.

"We're going to have to take turns, and it will be a lot easier with four of us than it would be with three."

She turned toward Harve. "Harve, you can take the early part of the night." Em knew Harve wasn't used to taking directions from his wife. She watched for his reaction, but there was none. "I'll take the wee hours," she continued, "and Matt and Em can divide up the daytime. Em glanced at Matt, but there was no reaction there either. Jenn was definitely doing what she did best.

"I will take care of cleaning and dressing her wounds," Jenn went on, "and fix what she wants to eat, but you'll need to fetch it to her and clean up after." This she directed toward Matt and Em. "Her pain pills are in the kitchen cupboard, and I'll put a paper and pencil up there so we can write down the time we give her one, so it won't be more often than every four hours." Jenn stopped here, seemingly pleased with her plan. "And the next person to take care of her will know when she had the last one."

Evidently confident that everything had been covered, she turned again toward Matt and Em. "Who wants the first shift to-day?" she asked.

Em waited, but Matt said nothing, so Em volunteered. Em got up from her place at the kitchen table and headed toward the parlor, but Jenn's next question stopped her. "Harve, what did the hired man want with you this morning?"

Em waited to hear the reply.

"Checking on Annie," he said. "Said the saddle cinch seemed to be a little off—may have had something to do with her fall. Said Doc told the boy how to clean the blood out of his seat covers." Harve's tone was matter-of-fact.

Em waited, but there was nothing else. She wondered again if it had been said that Matt rigged all the horses and if it was yet known that Annie was not on the dapple gray.

"I'm glad you didn't ask them in," Jenn said. "We're going to have our hands full here without company for a few days."

Em went to take her place in the parlor near Annie who was propped on the couch amid several pillows and who seemed to be sleeping soundly at the time, no doubt heavily under the influence of the morphine tablets.

Em looked around the parlor and saw that Jenn had done a good job. The parlor looked as efficient as a hospital room. The stand table she and Jenn had moved over by the couch had been outfitted with large and small wash basins, a pitcher, a glass, and a stack of clean cloths. Under the edge of the couch was the gray graniteware bedpan with a torn piece of sheet over it. Certainly Jenn didn't intend for Annie to stir from the couch. Jenn had situated a straight chair next to the couch, no doubt to make it easier for someone to hold the basin. But since Annie was so sound asleep, Em chose to sit across the room in one of the more comfortable parlor chairs. She opened a book, and when Jenn's voice startled her, she realized she must have dozed off.

"She won't be due for a pill until two o'clock," Jenn was saying from the doorway. "So she should sleep awhile yet." She came across the room and put her hand on Em's shoulder. "I know all this has been hard on you, too," she said. "Without your mother and all. Don't worry about dozing off. You'll hear her if she stirs. I just want someone in here with her." She patted Em again then turned to leave the room. "I need to get some cooking done, but you call me if you need me," she finished gently, heading out the parlor door and down the hall toward the kitchen.

Em wanted to call after her and say, "Did you know Annie was on the black horse?" but her mouth wouldn't open to let the words come out.

Matt came to take her turns sitting with Annie without saying a word to Em, and she was either in bed with her back turned when Em came to bed or she came in after she thought Em was asleep. She made herself scarce during the day and Em didn't really know where she went.

Everything about the brick house and the family seemed different now. Each person took a turn with Annie and then went about their business during the day. Even meals weren't taken together. Jenn made up what she called pot meals—soup beans or stew—and everyone dipped theirs up when they were ready or when they had time, along with cornbread squares and cottage cheese and pickled beets or whatever else could be found in the icebox.

The first two days passed with Annie kept heavily sedated by the morphine tablets. When she woke, she generally moaned and cried and sometimes retched and sometimes tried to take a little of the clear broth that Jenn had made up especially for her. She used the bedpan when she needed to, and she had not moved from the couch. Em began to worry that Annie was not strong enough to overcome this accident, and when Doc came to check up on Annie on the morning of the third day, Em overheard Jenn ask him if Annie shouldn't begin to rally by now.

"Well, ordinarily, I'd say yes," Doc replied, "but you know that little lady has never been too strong. If it was Matt, she'd probably be back on the horse by now, but you know this one's never been as sturdy." He put a hand on Jenn's shoulder. "She'll come around. She hasn't developed a fever, and that's a good sign." He tried to reassure Jenn, though Em noticed there wasn't the same confidence he had when he talked about setting the arm and cleaning the wounds.

Em felt out of place in the brick house now. Except for taking her turns with Annie, she tried to occupy herself by taking photos of the cats dressed in old baby clothes and by reading her books.

The boy and his friend stopped by on that morning of the third day, just a while after Doc left, and they spoke to Harve in the driveway. Em guessed they had come to inquire about Annie, and she saw that Harve was looking into the back seat of the Chevy and smiling at the boy, clapping him on the back. Evidently the blood had come out of the seat covers. Em wondered again if the black horse had been mentioned, but she didn't wait around in the kitchen to find out what the conversation had been about. Instead, she headed down the hall toward the bedroom to look for a book to take to the third floor. She wanted to choose a book that would take her far away from the old house and the strangeness of what was happening there.

Since it was Matt's turn to watch Annie, Em decided to make an important occasion of reading. She headed back to the kitchen and fixed a plate of cornbread and jelly and poured herself a cup of milk, glad that Jenn and Harve were outside talking to the hired man and his son who had stopped by again. She felt more comfortable about fixing things for herself in the kitchen when no one else was in there.

Em tucked her book under her arm and balanced her plate on top of her cup. This time, she decided to pass the narrow, winding back stairs nearest the kitchen and go up the broad front stairway in the entryway at the front of the house. As she moved down the hallway, she caught a glimpse through the parlor door and saw that Matt was busy working with Annie, doing something with her pillows—adjusting her pillows, Em thought.

Em stopped for a minute on the second floor to adjust her cornbread plate. It seemed like years ago that she and Matt and Annie had pretended to be princesses here—draped in old curtains, walking graciously around the room. Somehow she realized in that moment that it would not be the same again.

Em settled herself and her book and cornbread and milk in Annie's favorite place, in the tower on the third floor overlooking the front yard of the old brick house. She looked out the half-hexagon shaped window and saw that the hired man and his son were still in the drive talking to Harve and Jenn. Good of them to stop by, Em thought, though Jenn was adamant about not having anyone in the house to disturb Annie, and it was obvious Annie didn't have strength to see anyone yet. Anyway she was still sleeping most of the time, under the influence of the morphine.

Em watched until the hired man and his son left, looking for clues about what might be being said. Their truck was just turning out of the drive onto the road, and Em had just opened her book and taken the first bite of cornbread when she saw Matt running from the house toward Jenn and Harve. Matt spoke only a word or two before the three of them hurried back toward the house.

Em sat in the tower as if she was frozen. She couldn't move. In fact, she felt as if she wasn't even breathing. The piece of cornbread was stuck in her mouth. She couldn't swallow it, and she couldn't open her mouth to spit it out.

In a few moments she heard the wail. It was Jenn.

Em didn't go downstairs. She sat stone-still in the tower, in Annie's place, waiting for Doc's car to arrive. She didn't know how long she waited without moving, but when she saw Doc Whitney's car pull up the driveway, she still had the cornbread in her mouth.

MOTHER, DAUGHTER, SISTER

*S*ara felt the hard back of the chair against her head. Neither she nor Em spoke or looked at each other. Sara stared out the window, seeing the slightest perception of green on the big walnut tree. She pressed her head more firmly against the chair, trying to anchor herself in this time, in this day. She began to feel the tightness in her chest, and she thought she had not been breathing, so she consciously took one deep breath, then another.

"Are you all right?" Em spoke first.

Sara opened her mouth, and the words were hers, but they seemed to come from far away. "Are you telling me that my mother had something to do with Annie's death?"

"I don't know," Em stammered. "I just don't know that. I just don't know."

Sara looked across the table and saw that Em's eyes were pleading with her for some acceptance of "I don't know."

"Did you tell your mother this when she came home?" Sara asked, suddenly aware of the other woman's anguish.

"No. I never told anyone until now. At the time, I kept thinking that I must have misperceived things, that I was making too much of coincidences. Later, it seemed that the time had passed when I should have told things, and no one ever asked me . . ." Em's voice trailed off, and she looked again at Sara questioningly.

Sara looked back and nodded, as if to affirm.

The two women sat quietly for a long time, Sara staring out the window at the walnut tree and Em staring at her now-cold cup of tea.

The tree is very old, Sara thought. She looked again to see if she really saw the slight tinge of green at the tips of the branches. Yes, it was there, and she saw that a squirrel below was digging determinedly for some morsel that had been buried earlier.

"Would you tell me what happened after?" Sara asked. She realized she was no longer pushing her head against the back of the chair, and that her voice now seemed to come from herself. "Right after Annie died. Could you tell me what happened then?" Her voice was gentle; she was aware of Em's distressed state of mind.

"Nothing happened. Nothing did happen. That's just it. I didn't go downstairs while Doc was there. In fact, I couldn't move. I couldn't get myself to move. I was just vaguely aware of the hearse coming to get her, and I can tell you that Doc stayed during that time. It seemed to me that it all took place in a matter of minutes—from the time I saw Matt running from the house until I saw the hearse leave with her." Em paused. "But that couldn't be true, because it was getting dark when I was finally able to get up and start down from the third floor, and I know it was not that late in the afternoon when I went to the tower."

Sara sat quietly and waited. She wanted Em to continue if she could. She noticed that it had grown darker outside this old brick house now, and only the little light on the stove cast odd-shaped reflections around the room.

"When I got downstairs, she was already gone," Em said again, as if wanting to reassure herself. "Doc Whitney was gone too, so I didn't hear what he had to say about it. Jenn was sitting in her rocker in the kitchen; Harve was at the table, talking about what had to be done next. I went to the bedroom. I don't know where Matt was then. No one ever actually told me Annie died. Right away, people began to fill the house to help with things. Women were in the kitchen cooking, and in the parlor, putting everything back the way it had been before. Relatives came in . . . and the hired man and his family . . . and the boy and his friend. Some folks stayed overnight, sitting around the table, talking and drinking coffee. It was that way for three days, until the funeral." Em had been speaking in clipped sentences, as if she were in a hurry to get through these painful recollections.

"All I can remember everyone saying is something about the unfortunate accident, and Jenn and Harve said Doc figured it was a blood clot because of the deep wound on Annie's leg. That's just all I remember." Em stopped here and thought a moment then continued. "It was just a few days after the funeral that my parents came home, and I returned home. They just took the whole thing at face value, and I didn't say anything different. I guess I might have felt some responsibility or felt unsure of what I actually saw. I don't remember what. I remember that my father spent some time with me talking about the photos I had taken, but we didn't talk about the visit much beyond that." Em stopped.

"I never went there again," she said. "I always made excuses. But Matt came to our house a few times after that . . . with her parents. I just never felt comfortable with her again."

The walnut tree was silhouetted against the moonlight now.

Again, the two women sat for a long time without moving or speaking. For a while, Sara's mind seemed to be blank, with thoughts of nothing, neither the past nor the present nor the future. Finally, she moved her head slightly to look around at the patterns cast on the walls by the little light. It suddenly occurred to her that it seemed that she had been in this room many times before, many more times than she really had. She thought about the big kitchen in the old, white-frame farm house and about the noodles on the round oak table. She could feel the soft noodles in her hands as she swished them through the flour just as she knew the women before her had done. She saw the kitchen table in the brick house with Doc's black bag sitting on it, and she sensed the scent of the ether.

"Has the walnut tree been in the yard for a long time?" Sara was surprised at the words, as she didn't seem to think them before they came out of her mouth.

"It was fair-sized even when I was a child," Em said with a start. Sara guessed she had awakened her. "We always hulled the nuts in the fall for making Christmas candy." Em stopped here, evidently unsure of what to say next. She thought for a moment, then added. "We never did sit under it though, for obvious reasons. It's not the right kind of shade, and there was always the possibility that you'd get clunked by a falling walnut." She stopped again, as if waiting for Sara, then she got up to busy herself making hot water for tea.

Sara was looking at the tree against the moonlight. Finally, she spoke. "I've always envied people who had relationships with their mothers." She looked at Em as she put the tea in the pot to steep. "When you talk about your mother, and when you told me about Annie and Jenn making noodles and baking pies together, and about Jenn's mother making the big kitchen and giving Jenn the dresser set, it made me realize how much I've wanted to be part of all those things. I wanted to be somebody's daughter too. I wanted to have a mother, a mother like that." Sara stopped talking to keep from crying. "I've always wanted a mother."

Em was quiet awhile before she spoke. She poured some of the warm tea into Sara's cup and her own, then took a long, slow sip.

"Perhaps in much the same way that I've wanted a daughter or a sister," she said. "But there's something I finally figured out." She was looking gently at Sara now from across the softly lit table. "Mother. Daughter. Sister." Em sat her cup down. "It really doesn't matter." She was looking very carefully at Sara. "Mother, daughter, sister. They can be anyone you want them to be. They can be anyone—anyone you learn from. They can be anyone, Sara—even yourself."

"It's odd that you say that just now," Sara said, "because I was just thinking about Jenn and Annie making noodles and about the green dresser set and about how I can sit and comb my hair with that comb or look into the mirror and get a sense of the others." Sara was speaking very quickly, trying to get the ideas to work together before she lost them. "And about Matt, my mother—" She was continuing in a rush. "When you told me about Matt, I wasn't really horrified, in the way I thought I would be, but I could feel a sense of her pain, her pain at being left out, her pain at feeling she was rejected, different." She stopped again to catch her breath and to look earnestly at Em. "I could feel each one. I still can when I try. Am I making any sense at all? How can I possibly relate to my mother . . . when she did the things she did? This is not the way I expected to feel."

"But of course you can relate to them all," Em interjected, "be- cause you are part of them all—all the women who came before you and all the women who are living now. The noodle-maker, the mother, the hurt child, the daughter, the villain, the sister, the woman—you are part of them all. You were and you are."

"Do you know that I still have the farm?" Sara asked suddenly. Em shook her head.

"Well, I do. It was left to my mother, then to me. I've never lived there, never even gone there much, but I think I might live there." Sara was speaking softly now. "Of course, the house has been gone for years, but I could build a small place." Sara smiled. "Very small. And have a horse of my own. Not a horse to show, but just to ride. Just to ride around the farm at a trot."

Then, finally, there was nothing more to say. The women sat quietly for a long time, holding the warm tea cups, sipping the tea.

Eventually, Sara rose to go, and the two women stepped out onto the back porch into the purple-gray light that comes just be- fore dawn.

"Am I mistaken, or do you see a slight tinge of green on that walnut tree?" Sara asked, turning toward Em.

"Yes, you do see it. And I see it too."

X
NoR